Life AS A DRESSAGE TRAINER
IN THREE
COUNTRIES

A *Journey* Made Possible
by a Love for the Horse

GUNNAR OSTERGAARD

with Pam Stone

FOUR
IN HAND
▶▶◀◀
PRESS

AN IMPRINT OF TRAFALGAR SQUARE BOOKS, NORTH POMFRET, VERMONT

First published in 2023
by Four-In-Hand Press
an Imprint of Trafalgar Square Books
North Pomfret, Vermont 05053

ISBN: 978-1-64601-250-3
Library of Congress Control Number: 2023946944

Photos courtesy of the author unless otherwise noted.
Book cover and interior design by RM Didier

Typefaces: Eidetic Neo OT, Utile Display

Printed in the United States of America

10 9 8 7 6 5 4 3 2 1

To my father,
Eduard Ostergaard.

He didn't allow me to give up,
for which I am forever grateful.

CONTENTS

ACKNOWLEDGMENTS

To Germany

for giving me self-confidence for the first time in my 16-year-old life,
and for my *bereiter* education.

To Denmark

my native country, where I have strong roots.

To America

for its unlimited dreams and kindness.
(And to the old man at the Saranac Lake, New York, airport, in early
May 1976, who helped me with the payphone, put his hand on my
shoulder, and said, "Young man, you are welcome here!")

CHAPTER
1

ENDLESS MEMORIES

T HAD BEGUN AS A GETAWAY, later became our full-time residence, and now, in a handful of days, Birgit and I were obliged to pack up the remaining belongings within our beloved Vermont farmhouse—and home of nearly forty years.

I never grew tired of the view from our log and stone home. Here at the top of the mountain, the trees stand close together and the foliage changes from gloriously green to scarlet and then yellow, only to leave the branches twisting and skeletal for the winter, before the cycle of life once again begins the following spring. The gusting of wind is only interrupted by the sound of birdsong and the vocalizations of game found in the area. The horizon is endless.

There, just outside the front door, stood the stack of wood I had chopped up year after year. This was a chore I truly enjoyed, along with felling crooked and half-dead trees that would not survive anyway. There was a deep satisfaction in chopping them up and placing the pieces in a perfect stack of firewood. It is useful work, and I like the fact that I can easily see how far I have come. I would take a step back and look at the result, often flooded with memories of helping my grandfather Otto Andersen, who did exactly the same thing. I learned the technique from him and I still use it today. I like to think he would be proud of me.

Christmas Tree Farm Road...Birgit and I had both smiled at the charm of the name that had led us to the property, raw and undeveloped, all those years ago. Indeed, it had been a Christmas tree farm, an enormous 700 acres (of which we purchased the most usable portion of 245), although whatever was left had been completely overgrown when we first arrived. We had been looking for an "escape hatch," of sorts—a get-away haven in which to decompress after our busy schedules of teaching, training, and competing. And as we wound our way up the half-mile of twisting, rutted dirt road to the top, nothing could prepare us for the view as we stepped out of our realtor's car and drank in the seemingly endless panorama that encircled us.

It was little wonder that the town of Chester had denied planning permission to a developer who had ideas about carving up the entire 700-acre parcel and turning it into an upscale ski resort. It would be a sin, really, to do anything other than farm with this bounteous landscape.

As with horses, sometimes people choose with their hearts over their heads—after all, Birgit had always done our books, and had voiced concern over whether we could afford a second home, as we were still relatively new to America with an uncertain future. Yet after one look, she threw caution to the wind, looked at me, and said, "I think we should take it."

I immediately agreed with a resounding, "Yes!" And just as some experience with horses, our collective heads had a bit of a shock afterwards when we learned that there would be a hefty additional expense: it would be necessary for us to spend thousands just to bring electricity to the top of the hill where we planned to build our cabin. But what is money when one is in love? At least, that is what we told ourselves!

Glancing around one last time, I took in the stone walls—many had been overgrown upon our first viewing—and my eyes fell upon the creek, where further stones had been collected to add to what had been our solely timber home. Our builder, a fellow Scandinavian, had assured us he would realize our desire to be in by Christmas, and what a Christmas it was!

There had been four of us embarking on that jolly journey in 1981: Birgit; myself; our working student and friend, Lena; and another good friend, Peter. Of course, southern Vermont greeted us with a massive snowstorm, and halfway up our drive, my station wagon—German-made, but no four-wheel drive, and useless once snow topped its hubcaps—became well and truly stuck. Too filled with festive spirit to be deterred, we became pack mules of sorts, carrying everything four people would consider imperative to a proper Christmas: food, gifts, clothes...it took several trips slogging through the deep snow, but our mission was accomplished.

We were very good friends, but even friendship has its limits of intimacy; we entered the house to learn there were no interior doors, including the bathroom! We had been warned that the doors might not be delivered by Christmas, but somehow this had been forgotten amid all the excitement. As it was a small dwelling of 1100 square feet, it wasn't as though there were vast rooms in which to discreetly disappear and give anyone using the bathroom some privacy. And so out into the frozen night three of us would go whenever anyone needed to relieve themselves–which, considering how much red wine had been consumed, was often.

It was lovely to warm up again before the coziness of the all-important stone fireplace (we had insisted this be built using stones found on our property) as well as the good-sized Norwegian Jøtul wood burner near the dining room. We feasted Christmas Eve on typical Danish fare: duck, served with small potatoes, red cabbage, and lashings of gravy, washed down with more of the obligatory red wine. In those days, wine could often bring inspiration, and so it did with us–although I think the idea was manifested by me. We decided that come Christmas morning, we would take the red plastic toboggan down the long, steep hill in front of the house for a trial run. The fact that it was only technically Christmas morning–1:30 a.m, to be exact–seemed a trivial matter, and off blasted Peter, with Lena in front. None of us realized, of course, that a hard, frozen crust had formed on top of the snow, making the going rival that of a luge track.

Careening down the hill before the rapidly approaching woods, Peter knew he had to do something before the certain crash that would befall them, and so he stuck out his leg, with the same spontaneous conviction a mother uses when she throws her arm across the passenger seat to shield a child when braking suddenly. A human leg is no match for frozen snow while traveling at Mach III, and Peter did incur injury–but miraculously, no break, and as we helped him back indoors, he assured us that had he truly broken his leg, he would have told all and sundry that it had happened during a Vermont skiing trip while negotiating a black diamond slope.

So many memories...endless memories. Our first breathless arrival upon the closing of the farm at the office of Sarah Vail, who would become a lifelong friend in August of 1981. Living out of a parked RV, teetering at the very top, while exploring what we had purchased and working to clear the land together with both chainsaw and scythe. Wintering in Florida and spending summers in Vermont. My wonderfully understanding clients, particularly Ellin Dixon Miller, who appreciated why it was terribly important that we indeed compete at a dressage show in Woodstock, Vermont...

However, life comes with changes, and Birgit and I now had a farm in Denmark and had purchased a home in Tryon, North Carolina. We were spending less time in Vermont, and the upkeep—particularly in the winter when snow plows were required to clear the driveway—was a bit taxing. It was the autumn that we lived for with enthusiastic delight: the spectacular color of the sugar maples, and regular sightings of bobcats, moose, and bears.

That last morning, as we packed up our remaining belongings and walked through the house for the final inspection to ensure that its new owners would find all as it should be, we wondered whether it was purely coincidence that we were saying goodbye during a particularly splendid autumn. We took parting photographs of the sugar maples, looking as if they were in flames. And as we wound our way down that long, beautiful driveway for the last time, we were full of sentimentality, but no tears, for we both knew life has chapters—we were simply moving on, and in no way was this the end of our adventures.

Indeed, they seemed as stepping stones to a life I could have hardly imagined from the very first dream I held as a child in Denmark.

CHAPTER

2

EVER HUMBLE

N 1960, AT THE AGE OF THIRTEEN, I wrote in my diary, "Is there anything more beautiful than horses? Oh, how I love my horse Johnny."

Yet I was not born into a "horsey" family, nor did I come out of the womb half-halting between contractions and begging for a pony as soon as I could speak. My childhood was mostly a happy one, with parents who were intent on giving me the well-rounded foundation that was expected for any child of that era. This included dancing lessons (excruciating), piano lessons (less so), and scouting. However, when my interest in horses began to blossom, they attempted to distract me with something much smaller and far less expensive: budgies and homing pigeons. My father even built me a beautiful bird house for the pigeons, and for a while, this pursuit was interesting, as I would cycle miles away, a pigeon accompanying me in a small canvas bag, then release the bird and see how long it took to return home.

However, this could only placate me briefly, as I longed to be at the local riding academy where my friends were hanging out—mostly, in the beginning, to meet girls, but then to learn to ride. It was difficult not to feel left out and somewhat resentful, knowing everyone else was riding while I was tripping over my feet waltzing with a scowling young girl, and soon I rebelled, skipping my dancing lessons—still wearing the required dancing attire of white shirt and patent leather shoes—and cycling to the stable. I would return home to the ire of my mother, shoes scuffed and dusty, with the unmistakable odor of horses clinging to my hair and clothes.

However, if I were to pinpoint the exact moment I encountered my first horse, it would actually have been with my father, Eduard Østergaard. Born into a farming family with long and proud traditions, he grew up alongside the workhorses that would be driven to and from the fields, gathering the day's harvest.

I must have been six or seven when I was hoisted onto the back of one of the horses on my grandparents' farm. Broad-backed and eager to return to its stall after a day's work, the horse broke into a trot; I remember my father running alongside the animal, as if teaching a child to ride a bicycle for the first time without training wheels, and holding onto the horse as tightly as he was holding onto me. My head jounced up and down as my small body absorbed every shock of the jack-hammer, clattering trot. It was an exceedingly uncomfortable experience, and could not have been said to have ignited any sort of "horse fever" within me! I would, however, be exposed throughout those years to the sort of work ethic that would carry me through my entire riding career.

My father was the youngest of five children. In those days, it was traditional for the eldest to inherit the family farm. The next in line inherited money to buy his own farm. The next two in line—both girls—and my father inherited a mere 8 acres of forest to share. Looking back on the distribution, it was certainly not fair. Especially not for the younger ones. Yet feelings of inequality can sometimes trigger a competitive streak, and I believe this was true of Eduard Østergaard.

My father worked on various farms for three years and had thus received his agricultural training, but without a farm he had little use for his experience. He had to find something else to do, and he made the bold decision to move about nine miles away to the town of Haderslev, where he landed a job as a driver in a trucking company.

He found himself right at home, despite his rural background. When the elderly couple who owned the haulage company decided to retire, my father saw his opportunity and stepped in. He managed to buy the company and it proved to be a wise investment. In fact, he became more successful than either of his older brothers who had, respectively, inherited the family farm and inherited the money to buy a farm. I remember my father lending them money to help them through hard times more than once.

Eduard met my mother Betty, who had also grown up on a farm with dreams of expanded horizons, and they were married in 1944. In May of 1946, I was born, as part of the great generation of post-World War II children. I entered the world in Haderslev, which is only 31 miles from the German border. Haderslev had been part of Germany from 1864 to 1920, and during World War II, Denmark was occupied by Germany; the inhabitants of Haderslev included many people who were both German and Danish. It is difficult to imagine the overall feeling of those transitions, before and after the war, for the Danes.

My parents were hard-working people. Looking back, it is amazing to me that my father not only managed his small trucking company, but also "mucked in," driving the trucks, and loading and unloading them as well. My mother did the books, and every afternoon customers called for freight between Haderslev, Sønderborg, and Fredericia for the next day's run. My father's company drove between the three cities with two trucks that were always full of exciting things: machines, furniture, pianos, and even coffee and oranges, which were rare to see at the time because of the recent war.

My classmates were impressed by the big trucks and their contents. And so, I suppose, was I. When I wasn't at school, I went to work with my dad. It was his way of getting the next generation ready to take over.

My grandparents all had small farms just outside Haderslev. And although my father, who was a trained farmer, now owned a small trucking company, his interest in farming never left him, nor has it left me. There is a crystal-clear moment from my childhood that I can recall; I was sitting in the back of the car while my parents chatted about someone they knew who had become quite successful and had acquired large amounts of land in the area. The way in which they spoke of him, with respect bordering on reverence, created within me, that very moment, a certainty that owning land would be a wonderful thing. It represented security and a sense of fulfillment. And so, years later in Vermont, I engaged part of our property in sustainable farming, and later I made a respectable income from leasing 75 acres of hunting land I had purchased in Georgia, where cotton and peanuts were also grown. To this day, I find investing in real estate to be both enjoyable and exciting–particularly when it becomes a seller's market!

But in the years of my childhood, while my father could be quite frugal with things such as household expenses–which could spark sharp disagreements with my mother about how much she was allowed to spend on grocery shopping, or clothes for a growing boy–he could also be surprisingly generous. One of the most cherished memories of my youth, which still renders me emotional to recall, is the kindness my father extended to the residents of a local children's home.

These were children who had been either orphaned or removed by social services from abusive or neglectful households. I came to learn of them when, as a very young child, one of the first questions I can remember my mother asking my father was, "Are we going to see Didde and all the children today?"

Didde was a cousin of my father's and the manager of this children's home. An enormous woman whose size was only bested by her enormous heart, she ran a strict home with firm boundaries for children who had probably never experienced them, and yet there was a palpable feeling of warmth and joy when we visited, and I happily interacted with all the children–probably 20 to 25 of them.

It was an impressive red-brick building, set upon approximately 3 acres in a park-like setting, with swings and roundabouts on which the children could play. Having lost my younger sister at a very young age and feeling rather like an only child, these frequent visits were excitedly anticipated by me and were only trumped by the annual trip to the seaside.

My father–and it goes without saying that this was probably illegal–would bring his big, flex-freight truck with its tall metal framing and tarp covering to the home. Herding all of us within, he gave the strict warning that we must remain as quiet as church mice for the 45-minute drive to the borrowed beach house which awaited us. As was his custom, once we were no more than 10 minutes from the beach on the smaller roads leading to the house, he would honk his horn, giving us all permission to go wild.

Joining in giddily and feeling not only grateful to be a part of this happy group, but also hugely proud of my father's generosity, I helped rock that truck with the excited cheers of children as all of us—including me—blasted out the song, "We are the Children of Sun and Summer." Those trips meant the world to us, and it would be at that very same spot on the beach, decades later in 1978, where I would ask Birgit to marry me.

It was another one of these startling gestures of generosity from my father that brought my first horse, Johnny, the breathless topic of my diary entry, into my life. However, it must be said that while it was an enormous thing for a boy of 13 to be given a horse, I was most assuredly not to become the spoiled, privileged kid chauffeured to and fro from the riding academy. I had to cycle—everyone cycled—and was somewhat mortified to wear, day after day, the only pair of breeches I owned: a traditional dark brown pair I had received for Christmas, which ballooned out on either side of my thighs. As I was growing rapidly, it was not considered a wise investment to buy me a pair of properly fitted riding boots; instead, I could only hope no one would notice I was wearing my mother's mid-calf "scooter boots"—not unlike the American "go-go" boots of the 1960s.

All of this could have been forgiven had I not also been given a bicycle that I "would grow into," which was so ridiculously tall that my father attached wooden blocks to the pedals so I could reach them. It's a bit embarrassing to need a mounting block in order to get on a bike; why the girls at the barn didn't go wild for me, I'll never know! But anyone involved with horses learns quickly that they teach us to be ever humble, and this was certainly a way to swallow an early dose of humility. Evidently, that one dose wasn't quite enough, as nothing had prepared me for the horror I would experience when introduced to sing at the southern Jutland Coffee Table.

To explain: this "coffee table" was less a piece of furniture in front of a sofa and more an actual event, held at the farms of relatives—which certainly included a table, laden with cakes and endless cups of coffee—that was the weekend destination for my parents. Taking up much of the afternoon, it was a torturous requirement for which there was no means of escape, and I could only think about how all my other friends were at the barn, having great fun together, while I sat sorrowfully squashed between my aunts with crumbs of *Drømmekage* (traditional Danish "dream cake") around my mouth.

My parents, both graced with remarkable singing voices, were obliged to attend and genuinely enjoyed performing, and for me, it was non-negotiable. I was expected to join in this otherwise adults-only affair, and while it might have sounded enticing for a child to find himself before a sea of cake stands and try a sugary slice of everything, by the eighth cake, my belly was groaning and my belt too tight. Yet declining when one of the adults insisted, "Ah, go on, you must try this," was simply unacceptable. It is amazing to me that my teeth didn't fall out, and I didn't wind up needing a crane to be lifted onto my horse.

And, of course, there were no real conversations in which I could join these grown-ups, as the men gathered in one room, and the women withdrew to a smaller room with their knitting and homey topics that my mother, who was a bit more cosmopolitan than her relatives, abhorred. She wasn't the least bit interested in knitting or chatting about concerns of the hearth and home. In fact, she was the only woman in this group who went to the trouble to wear make-up and arrange her hair in the latest fashion. At one point, after doing the books for my father's business for years, my mother was approached by a friend about working part-time in a dress shop—for my mother, this was the gateway to sophistication. She adored it. And I suspect she may have been perceived as something rather exotic, or perhaps vaguely threatening; on one occasion I remember, while wearing a low-cut blouse, she was asked by my father's sister, with thinly veiled concern and a tight smile, "Betty, are you not freezing around your neck?"

My piano lessons had given me a bit of ability to play and, of course, I had to learn to sing. A cold chill still runs down my spine at the recollection of being pushed out, at the age of 12, in front of this small gathering to perform. With my cousin Else accompanying me on the piano, I attempted to croak out the German song "*Schlafe, mein Prinzchen, Schlafe Ein.*" My actual pronunciation was far better than my singing voice, although, truth be told, no one that evening could understand a word of my German. I wanted the floor boards to open and swallow me. I was certain that I could hear neighboring hounds in the distance baying with each note I "sang." Looking from face to face for some sign of encouragement, my desperate gaze only found the same confused expression that might be worn by dogs staring at a ceiling fan—utter perplexity. After what seemed an age, my mother deftly attempted to cover up my complete lack of talent by hastily explaining to all that I "certainly had a good voice," I just "hadn't yet learned how to hold a pitch." Which is like saying someone is a good rider, they just haven't yet learned how to get on a horse.

There was, however, a blessing attached to this experience. While my parents turned back to their adult conversations and my cousins were preoccupied with discussing *Popular Mechanics*, I took my chance and snuck out, unseen, to my uncle's stable.

In the late afternoon light stood a brown colt with the prettiest little star placed right in the middle of his forehead. This young horse had a reputation for being difficult—even a little crazy. But now, there he stood in the warm stable, smelling sweetly of horse, hay, and straw. It took me an hour to get a bridle on him, and the feeling when I succeeded was incomparable. That I could gain the trust of a horse on which everyone else had given up—indescribable! Little did I know then that I would experience that feeling over and over again.

In everyone's life, there are startling moments of clarity...epiphanies. And for me, as I turned to walk back toward the house that afternoon, there was a transformation—a deep knowledge within my very core that I had changed. That my love of horses had, as if someone had flicked on a switch, become all-encompassing.

I re-entered the house as a different person.

CHAPTER
3

JOHNNY

AFTER ONE OF MY FIRST LESSONS I nearly quit altogether. At that time, the actual riding hall was a good half-mile away from the stable, which was located at Haderslev Dam. This meant we had to—regardless of our level of experience—negotiate through streets and traffic on horseback until coming to the riding hall. Once I finally reached it, I was ordered back to the stable to retrieve a double bridle. Obviously, I had no idea what this was or what it looked like, and when I returned, carrying a leather strap I had grabbed at random and hoping for the best, I incurred the wrath of the instructor, and was told off in front of the other students. Things only got worse; then I proceeded to fall off on the very same discouraging day. Suddenly it didn't matter how cute the girls were; I was fed up after this disaster of a day and, tail between my legs, I cycled home.

Upon entering the house, I declared to my father that I was "never going back there again!"

Sometimes life lessons are learned the hard way, and shortly afterwards, I thought this might be one of those times, as my father became uncharacteristically furious.

"You can't just give up after your first lesson!" he barked. "You must finish what you start—this is the way it is in life. You are to go right back to the stable and schedule your next lesson, do you understand me?!"

It wasn't until years later that I learned the actual truth: my continuing to ride was far less about developing integrity and courage, and far more about economics. My money-conscious father had paid in advance for 10 riding lessons in order to get a discount, and had I quit, he wouldn't have gotten his money back!

I persevered and rode as much as I was allowed. When fall had passed, I was an enthusiastic rider, and by the time Christmas arrived, I was over the moon to receive my first pair of riding pants. Yet, as was typical of my dad, there was a note pinned to them, saying, "Not to be worn until spring." It was terrible for a child to have to wait that long—and perhaps the rule was compromised a little, for it wasn't long before I was turned out in my natty, balloon-thighed breeches, my mother's scooter boots, and mounted majestically upon my 17.2-hand bike, cycling madly to the barn.

Of course, nowadays I am indeed grateful that I did not bid goodbye to the equestrian world after that experience. And yes, it was an important lesson in not giving up. Although I certainly didn't agree with my father at the time, that challenging day was pivotal for the rest of my life. I became more and more enthusiastic about riding as my skills developed—any other hobbies I had as a child simply couldn't compare. Frustratingly, I wasn't fortunate enough to be given the opportunity to ride several different horses at the school because my weekends were fully scheduled and outside of my control. Other students were able to take advantage of mucking out and doing other chores at the barn to earn extra riding lessons.

Between being force-fed like a goose with Danish cakes on Saturdays and attending the dreaded dance and piano lessons, I only had time for one riding lesson a week, and it was difficult to watch Flemming, Torben, Peter, and the others soar past my own abilities when I so desperately wanted to do nothing but ride.

It was not long before my dream horse arrived. His name was Johnny, and he was an aged Knabstrupper, which, it must be said, had probably been sold to my father by the riding master with an overwhelming sense of relief. Johnny, with his inelegant head and traditional coloring—brown and black spots scattered over his white coat—had a well-earned reputation as utterly unsuitable as a school horse. He was far too spooky, and later on, it was only my fledgling skills as a dressage and jumper rider (we learned both in those days) that kept him manageable between seat and leg. In fact, we even went on to win a few shows, including three small combined winter competitions in low level dressage, earning us a heady mention in the local newspaper *Dannevirke.*

But in the unfailingly tight-fisted manner of my father, it was agreed that while Johnny would board at the riding school, my father would only pay for his stall. This meant weekly trips to my uncle's farm, where we would load hay and straw bedding into one of my father's trucks, to drive it back, unload it, and store it in the hayloft. I can well remember being at the barn and seeing that area roped off specifically for Johnny's groceries.

My father had learned to ride in his youth, in that sort of ramrod straight, "up-down" way of posting: gripping with the knees, with one hand on the reins and the other hand free to hold his cigar. So we shared rides on Johnny, with my father sometimes hacking through the forests, but more often enjoying riding through the city. I believe there was a bit of vanity involved—he rather enjoyed being the object of admiration.

I still smile when I think of how he rode out along Aabenraavej (a street in town) one fateful Sunday morning. Looking like a fashion plate from Abercrombie and Fitch, my father was quite dapper in his cap, brown boots, riding whip, and, trustingly, the reins in his left hand, cigar in his right. A hack to the harbor in Haderslev was what he had in mind, but Johnny had other ideas. As a horse that tended to move sideways more often than straight, Johnny may have had some Viking blood coursing through his veins—and so did my father, it was clear. What possessed him to choose to ride between the harbor and railroad tracks that morning, I'll never know, but off they went, with Johnny's eyes out on stalks as soon as he took note of the ships on the water. His heart thumping through his ribcage, he began to jig, and then, at the worst possible moment, a train rumbled past—and Johnny exploded. Terrorized between horse-eating ships on one side and an iron, smoke-spewing monster on the other, he plunged forward, and for the first time in his life, didn't go sideways, as he bolted and ran away with my father. Miraculously, they made it home in one piece, although my father lost his cap and cigar along the way.

During this time, I experienced my own sort of rodeo, but not on Johnny. As happens when one develops friendships with older kids, I rather hero-worshiped a boy named Flemming. He was only a couple of years older than me, at 15, yet he seemed worldly, brimming with confidence, and was wildly enthusiastic about riding because there were far more girls at the barn than boys. Come to think of it, that was one of the original motivations for my learning to ride, too, so I rarely hesitated to do his bidding.

During our cycling trips back and forth to the barn, we would pass a field not far from where we lived, which housed a grazing Fjord horse. Flemming had often talked about trying to ride it. "We should give it a go," he urged.

"I don't know," I replied.

"What, are you scared?" This was his foolproof way to get me to do anything. "C'mon, Gunnar, don't act like a little girl!"

With the typical reckless abandon of youth—we had no helmets, no idea how old this horse was, and we did not even know if he had ever been backed—we lured the pony to the fence and somehow managed to scramble on. It was Flemming's idea that he sit in the front, while I took the back seat behind him, probably directly on top of the animal's kidneys. The pony took a hesitant few steps before leaping forward with a succession of violent bucks, sending us flying through the air like rag dolls to land heavily on the ground. Shaking the dirt from our hair and ears, we had not a moment to lose as, to our horror, we saw the pony spin around, head lowered like a bull, and charge straight at us. We ran for our lives, and barely managed to scrape beneath the barbed wire fence, in the nick of time.

As we cycled home, we came to the conclusion that it was better to stick to the school horses at the barn and my own Johnny.

CHAPTER

4

WALTER FARLEY

I HAVE ALWAYS BEEN THE KIND OF PERSON who, when overwhelmingly inspired by something I've read or seen, wants to try it—at once. At the age of 14, while this applied to girls, mostly it applied to horses, and to any book written by the American author Walter Farley. But most of all, it applied to a riveting tale I had devoured, called *The Blood Bay Colt.*

This book was all about the world of harness racing, and it sounded enticingly glamorous and so vivid that, despite how well my riding lessons were going, I decided this was to be my path in life: I would become a world-class harness-racing driver and trainer. I would find a blood bay colt, just like the horse Gnisten in the book, and we'd win every race, every silver cup, and the newspapers would be filled with our success.

It's startling how some memories become rather hazy, while others are as clear as if they happened the day before. How well I remember realizing that career declaration as I stood in the schoolyard on my last day of school, in June of 1962, exhaling an enormous sigh of relief and saying, "Now, life begins."

School, you see, had been an unpleasant business for me since day one. I seemed to catch everything going around, missed a lot of school, and was forever trying to catch up. This resulted in the humiliation of quite a bit of bullying. All my friends were at the barn; I had none from school, and I had absolutely no intention of gaining further education. As far as I was concerned, the harness track was it for me. I even mentioned this to my first girlfriend, a sweet girl named Dorte

I had met at the riding school, in case she might get any ideas that I was planning what would be, to me, a boring, conventional life behind a desk. Alas, our budding romance never had a chance to truly develop; to my parents' chagrin, her father was a member of the Danish Communist Party, and in our small, gossipy town of 20,000, everyone knew this. Just imagine the cold, questioning looks and remarks from neighbors. We certainly couldn't hold a kid accountable for a father's actions, and Dorte and I did manage to sneak in a bit of time together, along with my friend Bjarke and his girlfriend at the time. We told our parents that in order to do well on our school exam, we needed peace and quiet to study, and this resulted in our being allowed to take our tents to Tomaj Beach—where the girls, of course, came to visit. But coming from a farming family, I wasn't sure how much we had in common when, during one of those visits, she asked whether cows really ate grass. Communism is one thing. Ignorance of animal husbandry is quite another!

Striking out with confidence, I lured Bjarke into coming with me on a bike ride from Haderslev to Odense, to check out the racetrack on Funen (the island on which the city of Odense lies). This was quite the excursion; we even took tents and decided to camp out. The place had a good reputation, and meeting the crowd that hung around the racecourse lived up to all my expectations. Filled with gusto fueled by happy anticipation, I cycled that round trip of 125 kilometers (75 miles) and, as soon as I returned home, sat down breathlessly to write a letter to Rudolf Jørgensen—a harness-racing driver who had been mentioned more than a few times in the press, and had won some notable races. When he promptly replied that I could start my training in August as a coach, I was beside myself with excitement. It was as if my entire life's path was being handed to me on a plate on my very first try, and I eagerly marked off each day on the calendar until the great date arrived.

Arrangements had been made for me to stay in a local boarding house, and my parents had given the place their approval. Incredible, today, to think parents would be so trusting as to let their teenage son, with zero experience away from home, go off to live with a group of complete strangers. But this was a different time; they had heard of Jørgensen, and it seemed very likely that I was being delivered into responsible hands.

Let's just say it didn't go nearly as planned. When I reported for work, I witnessed the first beer being cracked open at nine in the morning, followed by several others during the day. I was, frankly, surrounded by a crowd of barely functioning alcoholics, and even at that young age, I knew this behavior was entirely unprofessional. I kept my mouth shut for a while, and did as I was bid; however, after three months, when I asked when the paperwork required by the government to certify my training would be filled out, I was told they didn't have it, wouldn't have it, and that was that. In that heart-dropping moment. standing in that shabby stable office, I understood that the prospect of becoming more skilled and training harness horses was circling down the drain. Frustrated and despondent, I left and returned home to Haderslev, going to work for my father's trucking company.

There is a postscript to this somewhat depressing chapter in my youth. Much later, when I was an adult and living in America, I would experience an astonishing, full-circle conclusion to this story: Competing in Venice, Florida, not only did I win the Grand Prix, but the class was sponsored—impossible to believe—by Walter Farley, the very same author whose book had inspired me to try to pursue harness racing, who had become a resident of the "Sunshine State." It was extraordinary to have the privilege to shake his hand, as he presented me with the trophy during the mounted award ceremony. We later struck up a long and lovely friendship.

Oh, did I mention that the horse I was competing in that event was named Elektron? A black stallion...

CHAPTER
5

"ONLY GERMAN SPOKEN HERE"

THINGS HAPPEN, I TEND TO BELIEVE, for a reason—although it was difficult to see what that reason might be in this case, as I continued to help my father with his company after the fiasco in Funen. However, once I had sunk my teeth into attempting a career with horses, I was more determined than ever to try again.

Word had gotten around at my small riding club in Haderslev that a Danish rider, Nis Valdemar Hansen—who went only by his first two names, throughout his career—had also spent the bulk of his riding time at a small riding club in Denmark, but had finished his exam and become a professional dressage trainer while studying under renowned trainer and educator Karl Diel, in Flensburg, Germany.

This certainly caught my attention.

Leaving his local riding club at the relatively late age of 29, Nis Valdemar was able to follow his dream of immersing himself in dressage and becoming a professional thanks to the funds generated by a stroke of luck: gravel had been discovered in the ground on his farm, enabling it to become a lucrative quarry.

As I write this, I never hesitate to visit this wonderful trainer and friend—who is now 90 years young—when I return to Denmark. We enjoy sharing stories that leave us laughing until streams of tears pour down our cheeks. Back then, Nis Valdemar remained at Diel's for another year after I first arrived, and, being a distinguished *bereiter*, sat at the head of the dinner table, as was custom—with me, as the lowly "Cinderfella" apprentice, down at the far end by the gas stove. Yet we became great friends. As we were both Danes, he was careful not to show any special treatment or favor to me. We did, however, both receive the short, scorching side of Herr Diel's tongue when he happened upon us speaking Danish to each other: *"Hier wird nur deutsch gesprochen!"* ("Only German spoken here!")

Nis Valdemar's transformation while in Germany had been nothing short of remarkable. Prior to his departing for Diel's, he rode at what would be described as "country" level: affiliated with a small riding school, in a rural setting without access to a lot of sophisticated instruction, competing in local shows. Nis Valdemar enjoyed competing, but in those early days, somehow, he had not learned to feel whether or not a horse was on the correct lead. This had not deterred him from entering the show ring, as he had devised a plan to have a friend stationed outside the arena, whom he had instructed to raise up a small flag if he was on the wrong lead.

Obviously having improved by leaps and bounds, Nis Valdemar came to the end of our year together at Diel's and accepted an offer to lease a large riding facility in Aahus—Denmark's second largest city. It was here where he spent the bulk of his career, working to become one of our country's most successful trainers of all time. Clearly, he had learned his leads, as he took many horses (and riders) to Grand Prix level, including one of the Danish Team's horses for the 1984 Los Angeles Olympics.

Back in Denmark, hearing of Nis Valdemar's amazing metamorphosis lit a fire within me, and I knew in a flash that this was exactly what I wanted to do. This experience also serves as another example of the way I tend to develop a laser focus, when I am truly inspired by someone or something, until I achieve my goal. I decided, then and there, that I would get in touch with Diel and see if, by some happy chance, there might be an opening for a hard-working, dedicated young apprentice.

But how? I didn't speak German nearly well enough, and had no idea, in those days before the internet, how to get in contact with him. At that time, it was rather a big deal to make a telephone call from one country to another. It could entail having to sit for several minutes before hearing back from an operator that the call had been successfully placed.

It is rather amazing, in retrospect, to see a sort of "choreography" take shape across the course of our lifetimes: people weave in and out—people we might never really have noticed otherwise—until suddenly they become instrumental in shaping our futures. For me, hope arrived in the form of the kindness of Frau Frerks, a woman I would describe as a German with the heart of a Dane. Having lived in northern Germany for some time, she had followed her Danish heart back to Denmark, and, with her husband, bought the house my family had lived in until I was 10 years old. With her obviously fluent German and knowledge of the region where Karl Diel resided, Frau Frerks was sweetly enthusiastic in agreeing to help me, and knew exactly how to get in touch with Herr Diel. How well I remember sitting next to her, shaking with excitement, as I heard her make the arrangements with him to come visit my parents.

Clearly Karl Diel would want to see me ride, and so I put on my trusty brown breeches with their ballooning thighs for the car trip with my parents to Flensburg. However, upon arriving, it became apparent that there was no need to have prepared myself; I was never even put on a horse in that initial meeting. Instead, I was told to return on February 1st for a three-month probationary period.

Flensburg was a whole new world for me. To move from a town of roughly 20,000 to a city of 100,000 inhabitants was both startling and exciting. Flensburg was robust, noisy, and thriving. And the riding school, Flensburger Reit und Fahrverein, was located only a couple miles from the city center, in an area that was not otherwise characterized by rural surroundings. In fact, the riding school, attractive in itself, was surrounded by the multi-story buildings that were common in that era: gray, concrete, almost "Soviet bloc"-style architecture. My parents, ever supportive, had once again come with me to this new stable to help me settle in. And to our great surprise, Karl Diel was not even at home when we arrived. Evidently, it was not nearly as life-changing an experience for him to have another new student in the stable as it was for me and my family. Their hopeful expectations for coffee and conversation dashed, they could only wave goodbye and wish me luck as they departed, and I began to adjust to a new daily life in a new country.

It started with rather a shock.

Before my parents left, my mother had assured me that, as I would be studying under such an important man, I would probably get a nice room at the riding school. Nothing could be further from the truth. In Haderslev, I had had my own room in a house with central heating. Here in Flensburg, things were far more primitive. Not only was I to share a room with two others, but as the youngest student, it was my responsibility to keep the coal-burning fireplaces and stoves alight in the main rooms, the kitchen, and Herr Diel's office. It took me quite a few tries to learn how to do it. Yet, on the other hand, I quickly learned not to address anyone older than me by their first name. Karl Diel immediately became Herr Diel. Anything else was considered informal and rude.

In the evening, I helped the other three apprentices feed the horses, and received my own dinner, which was provided by the housekeeper Frau Wabbel. It consisted of fried potatoes and two thick slices of rye bread with sausage. If you were still hungry—and we always were—you were welcome to another portion of those damned fried potatoes. I will tell you now that if I never see another fried potato in my life, I will be a happy man. This was all we were ever served, for the full five years I lived in Flensburg under the thumb of Frau Wabbel. Breakfast had one purpose: to fill the stomach. It consisted of two slices of rye bread slathered in pork fat, and one slice with jam. We weren't even given plates with our meals, except for the fried potatoes. She tossed our food down upon the oilcloth that covered the kitchen table as if she were feeding a kennel full of dogs. Not exactly the "Breakfast of Champions." And coffee, considered far too expensive to be wasted on us, was replaced by tea—with sugar being out of the question.

Frau Wabbel was a refugee from East Germany, and in these early years of the 1960s, was used to having to turn every penny over. She was notoriously frugal, and was paid a daily sum to spend on feeding us young men. We suspected some of that money ended up in her own pocket, as she cunningly got day-old rye bread for free at the baker's, because she claimed it was for the horses. The food was certainly neither inspiring nor adequate. Even Nis Valdemar's uncle, well before I arrived, was served a terrible midday meal, to which he had been invited when he came to watch the horses being schooled. As if that wasn't bad enough, in the evening, the same meal was deposited in front of Nis Valdemar, because—according to Frau Wabbel—it was "only his uncle's leftovers." This "meal" went untouched for a second time.

I still remember when she served a dubious, chewy stew; later, to our horror, we learned the main ingredient in it was Edelmann, one of the riding school's horses who had just been put down. It's amazing that we ever-hungry boys didn't rebel, but when you're 16 and working a 12-hour day, you grab whatever is put in front of you. The only way to get a little extra on the plate was by doing extra hard work for Frau Wabbel. If you volunteered to sweep the cellar, do heavy garden work, or haul endless buckets of coal, you might be lucky enough to be rewarded with a fried egg slapped between two pieces of bread. Even that was a vast improvement on pork fat and jam. For the first time in my life, I missed the Southern Jutland Coffee Table.

The culture in Germany, I learned at once, was vastly different from that in Denmark. In Germany, there was a clear hierarchy that was not challenged. Ever. If Herr Diel said a wall was red, it was red; that was the way it was. We simply followed the rules and shut up, and I quickly found my place. It was easy to see what was expected of me, and it actually suited me quite well.

After a few days in Flensburg, Herr Diel returned from a riding competition, and it was finally time for him to see me ride. I sat on the back of a big mare named Laguna, without reins or stirrups, while one of the other riders kept control of the lunge line. Diel came out of his office and looked at me for five seconds before announcing that I looked like someone who had had an accident in my pants—although his actual words were much more crude. Then he left again.

It was not the start I had hoped for. For someone else, it might have been crushing, but it only made me more determined, and I didn't give up. I kept practicing, and spent loads of time watching a young man named Herbert Rehbein, the most talented riding student at the school. It was Herbert who, after three weeks, told me that Herr Diel liked my gutsy attitude. Those few words gave me the incentive and grit to try even harder. I shared a room with Herbert, and the two of us soon became friends. His help, needless to say, was invaluable.

Even though we were the same age—about 16 at the time—Herr Diel had already declared that he "could teach Herbert nothing," which was to say that Herbert was already that good, with the innate sense of feel that would later become his hallmark as a trainer, if not a legend, along with his ability to train one-tempi flying changes on anything with four legs. Eager to absorb his talent, I watched him ride every chance I had. Yes, there was no denying Herbert was a prodigy, but in those days he was also simply a boy, who loved nothing more than practical jokes. An incredible mimic, he would cheekily ride his horse behind a member of the public who had come for their weekly lesson—in particular, a hapless middle-aged man trying to learn to post the trot and repeatedly crushing his crotch against the pommel—and contort his body to look exactly like him. Of course the rest of us would behave disgracefully, aching with laughter while watching from behind the gate. Herbert could seemingly mimic anyone, and we encouraged him at every opportunity.

It was said that anyone who met Herr Diel would be informed by the man himself within 10 minutes that he had been the victim of a terrible horse-lorry accident, resulting in the breaking of no less than 21 bones below the waist. Forget riding, his doctors had told him; he would never walk again. He proved them wrong on both counts. Not only did he walk, albeit stiffly and always with the aid of a cane, but he could ride—and ride effectively. In fact, a competition highlight was his finishing 4th in the renowned Hamburg Dressage Derby. However, he couldn't mount on his own, and I was one of a few apprentices who were assigned to assist him with his very specific method: I would place one hand under his knee, the other would cup his foot, and then I would listen for his signal—"Hup, hup, HUP!"—before tossing him upwards into the saddle. Should I suffer the misfortune of misjudging my timing, I would then immediately suffer another, in the form of being cracked over the head with his cane. Perhaps that is what helped me become even more hard-headed with determination, over the years!

My days were spent keeping the stoves lit, feeding the horses, saddling up, riding, cleaning tack, and mucking the stables. In those days, horse-keeping was a far cry from what it is today. There were only a very few box stalls—about half a dozen for the elite horses—and all those horses who were privately owned stood in standing stalls, their halters attached to a lead with a ball at the end, which passed through a ring in the wall. This meant those horses could raise or lower their heads to eat and drink, but could not turn around. They were never turned out in paddocks. They stood in their stalls all day long, with the exception of our riding them for an hour, and on Fridays, an afternoon spent free-jumping. This sounds, I know, like a very unkind and inhumane way to keep a horse, and you might not believe me when I say that I cannot recall ever seeing these horses looking sour or depressed. And on top of this, a lame step was a rarity. They were kept side-by-side for company, with barriers in between, so perhaps being able to see each other, in addition to all the daily commotion in the barn aisle, kept them entertained. I can only speculate.

Cleaning their stalls was entirely different as well. They stood on straw, facing the backs of their stalls, which we cleaned daily by removing all the soiled bedding from behind them, forward, and in front of their front legs, before adding more fresh straw to the back, so they always stood on deep, clean bedding. Then, once a week on Fridays, we would strip the stalls, and a local man who farmed mushrooms would arrive in his truck to cart it all away.

On Sundays—and this still makes me smile—we were obliged to wear black jackets and bowler hats and ride to German marching music. I'm not exactly sure why this was mandatory; perhaps it was to remind us it was Sunday, and therefore more formal. And of course, none of us questioned anything, so round and round we worked our horses to the *"Deutschmeister Marsch"* and "Erika" until the order was given to reverse and work in the other direction.

When we traveled for horse shows, there was no such thing as temporary stalls at the competition venue, and no one tied their horses up to the sides of the vans during the day. Instead, there were rows of tall posts driven into the ground in front of a wall. The posts stood about four feet apart, with a chain attached, and this is where the horses would stand for the duration of the show, separated from each other by a single jumping rail. It would be difficult to imagine such conditions nowadays, but back then, it was all they—and we—knew.

Did the horses attempt to bite or kick at each other? Not to my recollection. And we riders? Did we bed down at a local hotel? Youth hostel? In our dreams. At the risk of sounding like a father wagging his finger at his children as he tells them of his childhood hardships, we slept on fold-out, army-style cots, with sleeping bags, a mere three feet behind our horses' hind legs. (On one occasion, at the Holsten-halle Neumunster February show, it was so bitterly cold that Herbert and I slept in one double sleeping bag in an attempt to keep warm). I will never forget the look of horror upon the faces of my parents when they arrived with friends to watch me compete at a show held in an old, converted livestock auction hall, and came upon our sleeping arrangements—directly behind the wrong end of a horse! Yet we were never kicked, nor, even worse, did we ever have a "deposit" left upon our heads.

Toward the end of my three-month probationary period, just as I was beginning to get comfortable in this new life in Flensburg, I woke up one morning feeling more ill than I ever had before. I looked in the mirror and saw, to my horror, that my face was covered in red spots. I had contracted measles, presumably from a family visit with my cousins, Hanne and Kim. However, I didn't know the German word for the disease, so I kept repeating *"Maeslinger! Maeslinger!"* in Danish, trying vainly to explain to my German friends what was wrong. Thinking I was babbling from delirium, the staff telephoned my parents to come pick me up and take me home to Haderslev until I recovered.

As I lay there in my bed, truly ill but relishing a break from pork fat and jam for breakfast, I was also terribly nervous, as the three months of probation were not technically over. Would I be approved? Would I be released and sent home, a failure? Once again, I got lucky. I recovered, quickly returned to Flensburg, and, to my great relief, passed my probationary period so that I could begin my career as an apprentice *bereiter*. Now, finally, my equestrian career would begin. At the relatively young age of 16, I had begun to adjust well to a new life, in a new country—in what would become a very long career.

CHAPTER
6

THE APPRENTICE

I WAS NOW WELL AND TRULY IMMERSED in my life as an apprentice. To earn the title of *bereiter* was an honorable distinction we were all working toward. However, what I was obliged to experience first was an admission ritual—also commonly known in America as "hazing"—in order to become part of the herd of apprentices at the *Flensburger Reit und Fahrverein.*

There were some terrific stories about Herbert Rehbein's admission ritual, which had been devised by none other than Frau Wabbel. She had convinced him he would be required to write and perform his own song during a celebratory party at the riding school. With her no-nonsense manner, she was so persuasive that Herbert wrote a song he titled, "Today Is the Day," and, in addition to singing it over and over in our room, he stood before her in the kitchen, day after day, belting out the bombastic verses and chorus until she could no longer conceal her laughter. Mercifully, she informed him he needn't actually sing, and had to reassure him that the party was only for fun.

These annual parties marked the end of hunt season, and consisted of an enormous banquet in honor of the sport's patron saint, Hubert. These jolly Saint Hubert affairs, the highlight of the year, were attended by my parents—now rather proud that their son had chosen the career path of becoming a *bereiter*—and were held in the actual stables. During the hunt, I had been honored with selection as the "fox," which meant riding ahead of 20 riders, deciding the course and tempo, so the celebration was even more festive for me. Aboard the exceptional jumper Gradus, who was pretty much life insurance for the job, I'd ridden the tempo as I had been advised to by Herr Diel—a soft medium canter, the kind I might have performed in the arena—while flying over whichever hurdles and ditches I chose.

Inside our "banquet hall," a long table would be placed down the barn aisle, elegantly adorned with vases of flowers, china, and wine glasses. The only dish served besides dessert was *erbensuppe und wurst*—that is, thick split pea soup with sausage—and, miracle of miracles, there was not a fried potato in sight! With this soup ladled out lavishly, for once our stomachs were satisfactorily filled, and it all went down beautifully with pilsners of Flensburger beer. And, of course, for the "digestion," this was followed by tulip glasses of Bommerlunder Aquavit—a Scandinavian favorite much like vodka, flavored with herbs. On either side, the horses had been reversed in their standing stalls so their heads would be looking out over our shoulders. St. Hubert might have been said to have miraculously healed a man from the bite of a rabid dog, but we didn't quite trust his ability to spare us from the decidedly powerful aroma of fresh droppings as we tucked into our *erbensuppe...*

As may be obvious after my disastrous singing debut at the Jutland Coffee Table, I was relieved to hear Herbert's "required" performance had only been proposed for fun. For my own admission ritual, I was instructed to open straw bales in a special way; it's possible to make it look like superpowers are involved, with a quick, powerful snap to break the baling twine. The secret is to turn the knots on the twine upwards. However, when I was presented with my bale, the knots had been discreetly turned backward, making it nearly impossible to break and leaving me looking like a 90-pound weakling, turning red in the face with effort and embarrassment, as the other apprentices kept straight faces and enjoyed the results of the prank. It was actually a bit disappointing to me that my "hazing" was only that—even though it took every bit of strength I had and several tries before I finally succeeded.

When the next student arrived, the bar was raised. We wickedly told him that Herr Diel was the chairman of the Salvation Army in Flensburg. This story was easy to "corroborate," for in the attic of the riding school, there were some Salvation Army uniforms, which had been left behind by a film crew that had filmed some of us riding the school horses for a documentary. The uniforms had big brass buttons, riding breeches like my old pair with the ballooned-out thighs, boots, and a hat. We managed to convince this poor kid to put on a uniform and go to a meeting out in town, thus giving Herr Diel a good first impression. We choked with laughter as he pulled on his uniform and boarded the bus into town, where the other passengers stared at him in wonder. We followed in the car, and put a stop to the joke before he reached the meeting. He took it surprisingly well. I'm not sure I would have kept my cool in the same way.

The riding school was for the elite class of Flensburg, who, in the 1960s, were elite thanks to their success in brewing beer and making alcohol. More than a few affluent business owners and their families had horses boarded with us. The chairman of the riding school owned the company Hermann G. Dethleffsen (now HGDF Familienholding GmbH & Co.), which produced the brandy Bommerlunder. However, the school's most significant client was the ambassador, known to us as Consul Petersen, who owned the Flensburger Brauerei. Together with his wife, he was always the guest of honor when parties were held at the riding school. Not surprisingly, copious amounts of alcohol would flow.

Consul Petersen was a tall, stiff, formidable figure, and someone that we boys, in a habitual sign of respect, were to doff our caps to in greeting. In fact, we tipped our caps to clients seemingly all day long. But when Petersen was in the barn, everyone walked a little straighter and was on guard for anything that might go amiss.

As apprentices, it was our job to warm up the horses for their owners so they were ready for lessons. It was verboten to talk to the horses' riders unless we were specifically asked a question. However, one day Consul Petersen's daughter walked past her horse in the stable and, thinking she was alone, patted it affectionately, murmuring, *"Tschuss, mein schatz."* ("Bye, my sweetheart.")

I, remaining crouched down where I had been applying liniment to its foreleg, coyly replied, *"Tschuss!"*

I don't exaggerate when I say I was very lucky to have gotten away with that.

When Consul Petersen was present, Herr Diel, whom we Danes would describe as "very German"—meaning sternly proper and disciplined—would become even more so. One of our unpopular jobs was to clean the toiletten. It had been my turn that week, and in my haste I had not been completely thorough, as Petersen declared loudly to Herr Diel upon re-emerging, "There is no paper in the toilette!"

What followed was a humiliating experience for a new student— an unpopular 29-year-old apprentice from southern Germany, who had earned the dubious distinction of being designated a "brown noser" by the rest of us. He tried to ingratiate himself to Herr Diel at every opportunity, including by washing Diel's office windows, even on his day off. Diel himself had seen through him, and disliked him intensely. However, this toilette episode was not his fault, it was mine, and yet he was harshly berated by Herr Diel, despite my trying to intervene and insist that it had been my fault, my oversight, and that the *arschküsser* wasn't to blame. There was an odd transformation that seemed to be taking place—I had begun to gain favor in Herr Diel's eyes. He had grown fond of me, and regardless of my efforts to save the new apprentice from his wrath, it was in vain.

CHAPTER
7

THE CIRCUS HORSE

CHAUSSEUR WAS THE ONLY HORSE at the school that was trained for Grand Prix. He was a large gelding—a mix of Hanoverian and Thoroughbred—owned by Consul Petersen. Herr Diel was in charge of his training, and rode Chausseur in competitions. The gelding could do some impressive flying changes and even piaffe—especially when it was from the ground and Herr Diel had the whip in his hand. Without the whip, though, was a different story, and while Herr Diel had been successful in competing the horse in Grand Prix, it was always the piaffe—or, rather, the lack of it—that prevented them from winning their class. But for me, on the occasions when I got to ride Chausseur, it felt like receiving dessert for my efforts.

In one memorable outing, we had all gone to one of the other riding schools in Flensburg, where some of the top German dressage judges had gathered for a forum to teach other judges how best to score the various Grand Prix movements.

This meant that multiple riders were to perform each movement in front of this panel of scrutinizing faces, and I was taking part aboard Chausseur. Soon, it was my turn to show various Grand Prix moves in front of over 40 German judges, on Consul Petersen's pride and joy—no pressure there! I was nervous, yes, yet I felt relatively confident and relaxed into the ride as my changes of lead went according to plan, as did the pirouettes and zigzag half-passes. All that was left was the piaffe, and, with conviction, I closed my legs. Nothing. Horrified, I squeezed with all my strength on either side of Chausseur, but he remained glued to the ground as if growing roots, so I squeezed again. I could physically feel my face changing color from sheer effort. Sweat began to trickle down the neck of my shirt, but there was absolutely nothing happening that even vaguely resembled the piaffe.

I didn't think it was possible, but my face turned even redder when I heard one of the top teaching judges, the highly respected General Niemarck, from Warendorf, turn to enquire of Herr Diel, "But the horse can piaffe, right?"

Herr Diel replied, "Of course! But the boy simply hasn't used his legs enough."

Herr Diel always said, *"Die beine zu machen!"* ("Use the legs!") if something needed to be improved. Horse on the forehand? *Use the legs!* Horse inattentive? *Use the legs!* Toilet clogged? *Use the legs!* And on this occasion, Herr Diel rose from his seat, walked up beside Chausseur's head, lifted his walking stick, and Chausseur piaffed like a dream. The very memory of that disastrous afternoon still makes me cringe.

My abilities, however, improved as I was given the opportunity to ride more and more good horses in Flensburg, and the memory of my beloved Johnny became a little less heartfelt.

It was not only dressage that was on the program in Flensburg. As an apprentice, I also had to learn to jump, and there were actually several good jumping horses in the stable. I learned a good lesson with Gradus: some horses, like people, do better in different careers. This gelding excelled at being quite difficult at dressage: he was hard-mouthed, very strong, and proved quite difficult to get on the bit, but on the show-jumping course it was as if he sprouted wings. While I savored being praised by Herr Diel for my dedicated work in getting Gradus round, comfortable, and straight, the horse's heart belonged in the show-jumping ring. Like a bay Pegasus, he flew over everything, including the winning high-jump round at a competition in Nordmark.

However, it was Diba, without a doubt, who meant the most to me and my career while I was in Flensburg. This six-year-old Hanoverian mare was sent to train with Herr Diel. She was one of those horses you got to ride if you deserved something special. The first time I sat on her was like going to heaven. She had a trot that looked impressive and was even comfortable to sit, and was easy to get on the bit, with a wonderful attitude toward working and learning. Being a part of Diba's training was like going on holiday. Together, we won a Medium-level test, held in Leck, not far from Flensburg, and the prize awarded was silverware for six people in a beautiful rosewood box, lined in soft green velvet. My parents were rather impressed when I brought home this prize—which was far more useful than a trophy to put on the mantelpiece. (I still have that cherished box of silverware, which we use when we have guests for dinner.)

Diba was also my partner for a large show held at Stadthalle Bremen, which was a heady experience indeed. I was 19; this was my first attempt at the more demanding S-level class, with its pirouettes, zigzags, and flying changes. And while I did not come home with a rosette, it became a halcyon moment in my life. Before that, I had won a rather large M-level class with Fritz Thidemann judging.

Although Diba was a dream to ride, it was very difficult to put a bridle on her. It's ironic to me that my first jubilant moment with horses was the triumph of bridling that other difficult youngster in the barn when I snuck out of the monotonous Jutland Coffee Table during my childhood, yet here I was, years later, an apprentice of Karl Diel's with multiple competition successes, unable to bridle this wonderful mare! We tried every possible way to solve the problem, with little success. We lured her with sugar, we tried to distract her, and we even tried to pry her mouth open. But nothing helped. It was a mystery to me that this horse, so wonderful to ride, found it so difficult to accept bridling.

And then there was the "Circus Horse"...

In the autumn of 1966, an exceptionally handsome gray stallion named Rhenus, with a fantastic dressage pedigree, arrived at the stable. The task was to get him ready to perform in a Danish circus that was traveling around Norway. This sounded both glamorous and exotic to a young man like me. Rhenus had to learn the piaffe, the passage, and the so-called Spanish walk—exercises that would look impressive in a circus arena.

Rhenus was bright, and quickly learned these new exercises. I sat on his back while Herr Diel walked beside him with his whip and pockets full of sugar, as Rhenus learned the Spanish walk. Every time Herr Diel prodded one of the horse's front legs, it had to be lifted far up and forward. As the rider, I was to slide my corresponding leg forward and lift the rein, then alternate with my other side, as Herr Diel tapped the other leg. Rhenus was a marvelous student, and this training proved to be a breeze.

One thing Rhenus didn't need any help learning, however, was how to buck. Here, he would have fit better into a rodeo than a circus, and his explosions were legendary. I've never sat on a horse that could buck like him since.

To the great amusement of everyone but me, he repeatedly succeeded in bucking me off. And not just once. Over and over again. The record was eight times in one hour. Herr Diel left the riding hall while I lay on my back, motionless, the wind knocked out of me, trying to catch my breath. When Herr Diel came back, he was clearly surprised and slightly exasperated that I was "still lying there and messing around." The truth was that I had remounted, and had then been launched from the saddle yet again before he had returned. Others tried their luck, and even the *arschküsser* apprentice became temporarily airborne, but to no avail. It was a good month or two before I figured out that the trick was to make sure Rhenus didn't dive his head down between his front legs. That way he couldn't buck. And so when he would try his clever trick of plunging his head downwards before blast-off, I would stick my hand forward and give a sharp, upward jerk on the rein to keep him from doing it. This required me to stay one step ahead at all times, and when Rhenus realized I'd figured him out, he was smart enough to stop.

Rhenus was owned by Viola Mundeling, who, appropriately enough, was also a circus princess. She came to visit to watch the horse's training. I warmed up Rhenus, and, as I held my breath watching, he actually managed to behave himself while she rode him.

When spring came again, Herr Diel judged that Rhenus was ready for the circus. It was a journey I will never forget.

The destination would be Bergen, in Norway, where Cirkus Löwe was based—a trip of about 620 miles (almost 1,000 km). Our first vehicle was the horse trailer, to convey us from the riding school to the train station. At the station, my gray traveling companion and I switched to a freight car on the train, with hay, feed, and my suitcase. We may have been the only passengers in this train car, which was full of the lovely smell of hay, but that was the only luxury. Here, I had to sit on my suitcase, where my backside absorbed every lurching jolt of the train for what seemed an eternity, with only a horse for company. There was no view to take in to pass the time, as there was only half of a window, and it was set above the door, too high for me to see out. That is how I traveled, for 9 bum-numbing hours. I was so relieved when the trip ended that it hadn't occurred to me to worry about what might await us after we arrived in Frederikshavn, but it certainly wasn't a horse trailer. To my horror, after I led Rhenus off the train and asked the way to the ferry from a bemused porter, I realized we would have to proceed on foot. This meant leading Rhenus through evening traffic, in the rain, carrying my suitcase in my other hand. Bits of hay sticking to my sweater and trousers completed my bedraggled ensemble. Show business!

When at last we reached the ferry, a somewhat primitive stable had been built for Rhenus on the car deck, while I had to be content to stay nearby in a small, spartan cabin. But I was nervous about his well-being and checked on him constantly during the night. Amazing that no one had even considered a horse might colic under these circumstances—in a makeshift box wedged between enormous trucks and passenger cars. Rhenus didn't, thankfully, but that was how my next 11 hours were spent: on a ferry heading to Norway, again with a horse for company, and definitely the talk of the rest of the passengers. Rhenus steadily munched his hay, and I took advantage of the ferry's restaurant, relieved to at least have a decent meal, as all I had had to munch on during the train ride had been a couple of sandwiches I had made while Frau Wabbel was out at the shops, busy extracting more free bread for the "horses" from the bakery.

The trip felt endless, and I think we were both tired of the relentless rain. But when we finally arrived in Bergen, we were welcomed by the entire circus family. All of this was a glittering and intoxicating affair for a young man like me, who had never experienced the circus. Rhenus was given a comfortable box, and I was assigned my very own circus trailer in which to sleep. I was relieved that I didn't have to share a trailer with the sword swallower; he had split his pants open upon sitting down, and was off having them repaired.

My travel companion and I quickly found our feet among performers, clowns, circus princesses, and strongmen. I was truly a fish out of water, dazzled by the company. I had brought my nicest outfit because I was expected to show off all the new tricks Rhenus had learned in Flensburg, and everyone was duly impressed as Rhenus bowed low, at the same time that I took off my hat and bowed low. I had only a couple of days to practice before my first performance, and into the little round arena we went, working on the Spanish walk, a bit of piaffe, passage, and pirouettes—who cared if the pirouettes weren't perfectly balanced around the inside hind leg? A sure applause-getter was our final bow before the crowd, in which I also removed my bowler hat. To think I was performing in the circus in front of a packed audience—now this was show business! The icing on the cake was seeing Rhenus and myself in a terrific photo published in the Bergen newspaper.

But my responsibilities were far from over, as it was Viola who was to perform with Rhenus—and, thankfully, they were successful beyond all expectations. It was as if Rhenus had forgotten his greatest trick of bucking his riders into orbit. So, after a few more days as a member of Circus Löwe, I waved goodbye to my traveling companion and my new friends, and returned to Flensburg to my everyday life as a now-distinguished *bereiter*, still riding the high of our success.

Three weeks later, a telegram arrived from the circus.

Viola was bucked off during a performance STOP
Come back as soon as possible STOP

Although it was not good for either Viola or the circus that Rhenus had started to remember his misdeeds, I was secretly quite excited at the prospect of once again becoming part of Circus Löwe.

And this time, the journey was far more pleasant. I even got to travel first-class on the train, and I had my own cabin on the ferry. When I arrived in Oslo, there was not a circus carriage waiting for me, but a lovely room in a lovely hotel. Clearly, being a horse trainer in a circus had lavish perks—the greatest one being not a trace of pork dripping or fried potatoes.

I rode Rhenus a few times, and knowing I was in the saddle and wise to his tricks, he again behaved in an exemplary manner. Not the slightest sign of sticking his head between his forelegs to get his butt in the air. I stuck around long enough to confirm that he remained obedient with Viola before returning to Flensburg, and happily, it didn't take long.

However, a little later in the year, his bucking started to show up again. This time, the circus princess had had enough of being launched into the air without a net, and she sent Rhenus to Flensburg to be sold. Circus Löwe later changed its name to Cirkus Viola Mundeling. Whether this had anything to do with her aerial tours thanks to Rhenus, we never knew.

But now my travel companion was back with me, and he was feeling content in this arena. Rhenus was a wonderful mover, had an ease with flying changes, and was what I would call a "smart model." We had success at horse shows, and then Herr Diel had the sudden idea to try him at jumping, thinking a career change might cure his bucking—and what a career change it was. Rhenus took to show jumping like a duck to water, and together, we won an exhilarating jump-off in which the fences reached just over 6 feet. This was a euphoric moment for me. However, it wasn't long after this success that Rhenus was sold on to a well-known German dressage rider, and that was the last I saw of my circus horse. But I heard later that he had bucked off the owner, who then sold him on again. It's a shame Rhenus was born during the wrong era and on the wrong continent—he would have made the perfect template for a mechanical bull.

There are times when I think many horsemen and horsewomen look back and wince at the memories of seemingly reckless things we did with horses in our youth, whether it was thanks to lack of experience or simply because that was the way things were. And while

Rhenus could be very naughty with his bucking, when I think of how trustingly that horse followed me through the traffic-congested streets of Frederikshavn, stood quietly in his rickety box overnight on the ferry, toured with the circus (and gave me the opportunity to perform in the circus as well!), not to mention soared triumphantly over six-foot jumps, well, what a gem of a horse he was.

Every year my father made 25 orphan children very happy with a beach trip in this truck.

Taken in 1977 at the Empire State Building: my mother, on her first trip to the United States.

The Reitschule in Flensburg, Germany, where I spent five years: three as an apprentice, and two as an assistant trainer.

Five apprentices of Karl Diel: from left to right, Frederic Warnholc, me, Hans Ulrich Harnack, the legendary Herbert Rehbein (wearing the cap), and Franc Helmke.

This mare, Diba, meant the most to me during my years in Germany, and taught me a great deal. I did my first S-level dressage with her at Stadthalle Bremen, when I was 19. *Photo by Foto Göhler*

I left Denmark for Germany at age 16, and was the youngest apprentice at Karl Diel's facility when I started.

Karl Diel is in the center here; I am in the red hunt coat.

Peter Boeck, Franz Helmke, and Bodo Chromick demonstrating
their trust in me...or perhaps their trust in the horse
I was riding, the great jumper Gradus.

At the Reitschule in Flensburg, a barn aisle dinner in honor of St. Hubert. The horses in standing stalls were turned around, for good reason.

Frederiksdal Castle, home to the riding facility north of Copenhagen where I worked for seven years before emigrating to the United States.

The Frederiksdal Castle outbuildings had been converted into a stabling for 25 horses.

Fellow student Ina Zetterstrom and I in 1970-71, at an exhibition at Frederiksdal.

Winning at professional puissance (high-jumping) in 1972, at Barthahus in Denmark. Here, my horse Tonka and I are jumping 1.95 meters (6' 4")—notice the wooden beer crates that were needed to raise the jump.

In 1975, celebrating a very happy win just prior to emigrating from Denmark. This was at the Danish Professional Trainers' Association anniversary show; the top four finalists exchanged horses, with three minutes to warm up on their new mounts before the Prix St. George.

An unforgettable day: on April 22, 1976, my mentor Gunnar Andersen and my great friend Ina Zetterstrom saw me off from Copenhagen Airport, before I departed for the United States.

The seven Conroy sisters and brothers, photographed in Plattsburgh, New York. Peggy (on the left) and John (second from right), along with John's wife Liz, sponsored my green card. I will forever be grateful to them, and we remain friends to this day.

I used this photo for my only advertisement after immigrating to the United States: a two-time ad that ran in the national horse publication *Dressage & Combined Training*.

Some of my early US clinics were held at the magnificent "Great Island" estate, which belonged to Sis and Bill Steinkraus.

At an exhibition in a packed Madison Square Garden with Edith Masters, in November 1977. We received a standing ovation.

Edith and I had fun at "The Garden"! My tailcoat (borrowed from Sis Steinkraus) was a bit short.

I had early FEI wins on Elizabeth Madlener's Jonathan Swift, sent for training all the way from the state of Washington.

My wedding at Horsholm Church in Denmark, April 1978, with a completely unexpected surprise for the happy couple: when Birgit and I exited the church, there was a beautiful four-in-hand carriage, with an escort of 16 horses with riders clad in red jackets, to take us to the Hotel Marina for our reception.

Birgit and I during a ride on Mr. F. Eugene Dixon's 500-acre Erdenheim Farm, on the Philadelphia city line; we moved there from Long Valley, New Jersey. *Photo by Jurgen Bak Rasmussen*

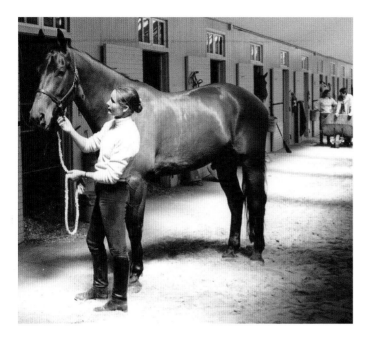

Birgit in our barn at Erdenheim Farm, which was a former racing stable where an indoor racetrack surrounded the stalls.
Photo by Jurgen Bak Rasmussen

This photo is from 1983; Ellin Dixon Miller is on Erebus, and I am on Elektron, the horse with whom I won the Grand Prix at Devon twice.

Mr. Dixon's horse Lynnewood Hall started his career as a racehorse, and then became a jumper for Michael Matz. I took him to Prix St. George before he was sold to my friend Raul de Leon. *Photo by David Gillmor*

A great day in our early marriage: Birgit and I bought the first of several locations we would name "Deerwood Farm." This one was in Quakertown, Pennsylvania, about a 40-minute drive from Erdenheim Farm. It was our first time ever owning real estate; a stone farmhouse was our dream, and we'd looked for years before we found our first "Deerwood."

Ellin's first Grand Prix horse, Bit O'Shine ("Bits"). I had great respect for how Chuck Grant trained this horse.

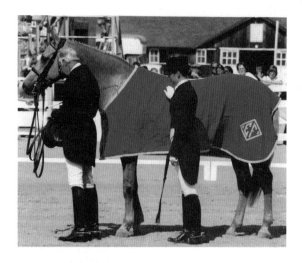

Bits and I participated in a miniature street exhibition in front of the Philadelphia Children's Hospital. I hope I lightened those children's lives, at least for a little while.

Ellin Dixon became a National Grand Prix champion on Chigwell in 1981.
Photo by Cappy Jackson

CHAPTER

8

WARENDORF

THERE ARE PLACES IN THE WORLD where, even if a sport is unknown to any given individual, the very name still conjures up hallowed ground. *Wimbledon...Augusta...*and, for the equestrian, *Aachen*, Germany. And—also in Germany—for those who wanted to achieve the position of official *bereiter*, there was only one place: *Warendorf*. Indeed, it was Warendorf which was to be my destination; specifically, *Die Deutsche Reitschule*, as I traveled by train from Flensburg with my fellow apprentice of three years, Hans Ulrich Harnack.

The time had arrived to take the exam which would determine whether we would receive the accreditation necessary to embark upon a professional equestrian career. Being 19 and well trained, I felt reasonably confident in my ability to ride the required Medium-difficulty dressage test and the 4-foot (1.25-meter) show-jumping course—even the written test on theory was not daunting. But the speech we were to give before a panel of German officials brought back stomach-churning memories of being pushed out to sing in front of bewildered relatives at the Jutland Coffee Table. This requirement made perfect sense: the officials wanted to see how we presented ourselves in a relatively brief speech about our background, abilities, and aspirations. We were hoping to become professionals, and it was only natural we should have the ability to present ourselves as such.

My nerves seemed only to heighten upon entering through the enormous oaken doors of the equally enormous brick building of the Reitschule. I lurched between awe and intimidation—the facility went on seemingly forever, with vast barns and indoor and outdoor arenas, surrounded by acres of manicured countryside...it was everything I had imagined and more.

The exam would be taken over a period of three days and conclude on the fourth, when a modest reception would be held during which all of the candidates—around twenty or so, I recall—would learn whether they would earn the certificate which would help them launch their careers.

Checking in to my room later that afternoon, I pored over my speech, the result of three weeks agonizing over each word, practicing in the mirror, and taking frequent sips of water to lubricate my throat, which felt dry with nervous anticipation. Taking a break, I dug out my diary—a horse management journal each candidate was to have kept up to date, showing our organizational abilities in scheduling lessons, training, ordering hay, and managing veterinarian and farrier appointments; in short, everything that is considered necessary in running a professional stable. Having been impressed by my grandfather, who used red ink in all his business correspondence, I too had obtained a fountain pen with red ink, which I felt made my journal look equally significant. However, it took some doing to categorize and write up everything properly in formal German. Here, I was lucky, in that my on-again-off-again girlfriend at the time, Krista, had a precise command of German, and she was instrumental in helping me rewrite the thing until it was satisfactory to us both.

Krista and I had met when I trained both her and her horse at Flensburg. This was the source of a few raised eyebrows at the barn. In fact, it's possible that our courtship was the first time such a thing had occurred at Herr Diel's, as speaking to clients unless spoken to was frowned upon, so the thought of actually dating one had seemed as unlikely as landing on the moon. The fact that she was from an exceedingly wealthy family made things even more intriguing. We were secretive in our meetings; I can remember us holding hands on the street one day, only to jerk away from each other upon seeing Herr Diel drive past us in his Volkswagen.

He never said anything about it, and I will even speculate that perhaps, considering her family wealth, he thought this might prove to be a beneficial match! However, while man did indeed land on the moon a short time later, our relationship didn't last. Still, on those occasions when we were "on again," Krista had been both helpful and supportive, even courageous, to accompany me, buzzing along in my trusty red VW Beetle.

The night before the test, I slept surprisingly well despite my nervousness, and in the morning I ate lightly—the last thing I wanted was the feeling of a bellyful of weisswurst as my name was called for my presentation.

Our group assembled in a large room where chairs had been set up for us to sit, behind the semi-circle of six seats for the members of the panel. While our view would be the backs of these austere gentlemen, their view would include the glass cases housing the multitude of Olympic and World Championship medals and glinting trophies won by generations of German riders, as well as each presenter's panic-stricken face. When it came time for my presentation, I straightened my narrow tie, cleared my throat, and walked up to stand before those imposing glass cases, facing the men who would determine my fate as I began, in a loud, clear voice, to give my succinct *lebenslauf*:

> "I, Gunnar Ostergaard, was born on May 16th, 1946, as the son of the owner of Östergaard Freight Company, Eduard Ostergaard, and his wife, Betty, in the town of Haderslev, in Denmark."

My eyes swept the panel for any show of encouragement. There was none. They didn't even blink. It was like staring into the eyes of the big stone heads on Easter Island. They were expressionless.

I continued, my heart thudding beneath my tweed jacket.

> "I started my education at the Hertug Hans School in 1953, and after nine years, I finished in 1962. I continued my riding lessons and activities at the local riding school in Haderslev, and during the summer, I started to work for my father at his business."

I swallowed, wanting a sip of water, and tried to ignore my dry mouth. In my nervousness, I feared I would be inclined to rush the rest of it in my desire to get it over with, and so to remain in control, I spoke even louder, in formal German, sounding like an army cadet barking out his name, rank, and serial number.

"I WAS ACCEPTED TO BECOME A *BEREITER* APPRENTICE BY HERR KARL DIEL AT THE *FLENSBURGER REIT UND FAHRVEREIN*, AND STARTED MY THREE-YEAR EDUCATION ON FEBRUARY 1st, 1963. IT IS MY HOPE AND GOAL TO ADVANCE MYSELF TO THE BEST OF MY ABILITY, AND TO RETURN TO WARENDORF IN FIVE YEARS TO PASS MY EXAM AS A *REITLEHRER.*"

There were no smiles, and certainly no applause, but probably profound relief when I finished. I was dismissed by a curt nod of the head from the official seated in the center, and I returned meekly to my seat. Looking back on that very short biography of my life, it is funny that I labored so diligently over it for weeks.

The following day, our exam continued with a test of our knowledge of theory—not terribly difficult for me—and the last day was devoted to our ability in the saddle. We were given specific horses on which to perform a Medium-difficulty dressage test, including all the lateral movements at trot and canter (shoulder-in, travers, renvers, half-pass, and flying changes); and later that afternoon, our prowess in riding a show-jumping course on another assigned horse would be scrutinized. I had few concerns regarding the jumping—while dressage was my passion, I thoroughly enjoyed jumping, and was lucky enough to draw a horse owned by a well-known show jumper—but my first thought upon mounting the nondescript bay gelding for the dressage test was, "Boy, what a lousy mover!" And, of course, that was the point. I'd been privileged to ride some quite nice horses at Flensburg, but as far as the examiners were concerned, a well-trained young rider should be able to take a mediocre horse and improve his way of going.

This I managed to do, and while I felt relatively confident when it was all over that I had passed the exam, all of us held our collective breath until the next day, during the reception, when the names of each candidate who had earned the title of *bereiter* would be called out. Everyone passed, which was lovely, and I was happy to finish in the top 10. It was actually a closer competition than it sounds, as the fellow who was top of the class had indeed earned a high score, but the rest of us who followed all had the same score, finishing second, as if someone had won a dressage class with a 75 percent and the next several riders all scored 70 percent. And so it was with a certain amount of pride and accomplishment that I stepped up and received my certificate. After all these years, I still have it, and it hangs, framed, in pride of place on my office wall.

The first perk of passing the *bereiter* exam was an immediate improvement in travel arrangements—while I had taken the train up to Warendorf, I was driven back by Herr Diel, in his funny, square Volkswagen 1500, which he affectionately referred to as "the devil," as he liked to point out that it had a far more powerful engine than the common Beetle.

As the car took a full 20 seconds to trundle up to 60 mph, I'm not quite sure how it earned such lavish praise, but I certainly had ample time to fill in Herr Diel on my entire exam experience as it climbed to its top cruising speed of 78 mph.

By the time the spring of 1968 rolled around, I had been at Flensburg for five years, and I had thoroughly enjoyed myself. I had a title I could be proud of, and while Flensburg had built character and prepared me well for my future, I knew there was little more I could learn there. It was time to spread my wings. I began looking for my first job.

Quite quickly, I was offered a job back in Denmark, at Herning. In those days, riding schools were often run by a board of directors who tended to have little knowledge of horses. The place was impressive, but the job description included a mountain of administrative work: running the riding school, organizing lessons. And while I would be given the opportunity to train privately-owned horses, the thought of spending half the day being a paper pusher who was accountable to the board filled me with dread. Far too much like a "desk job." I politely declined.

Little did I know that in the meantime, Herr Diel had been casting his net for a future position for me. The year before, I had brought up the idea that it was perhaps time for me to move on, but it was a full six months before an opportunity presented itself. That fine summer day remains etched in my memory. We were leaning against the top rail of the arena, watching a horse and rider work, when a phone call came through, seeking a *bereiter* for a potential new job. It was a couple in their 60s who had built both a successful clothing business in southern Germany and an equally impressive riding facility for their own horses. They were hobbyists—they weren't looking to go to the Olympics or build a massive training facility, but they were searching for someone who could train the horses they had, and perhaps take in a few more so that the place would essentially pay for itself. Herr Diel thought I would be the ideal candidate for such a position.

As we stood by the arena, I had the distinct impression that he wanted to speak, but found himself unable. It took two or three attempts before he was able to explain the offer of this position, and then, in the middle of a sentence, he reached up to blink and—I assumed—rub away something that had gotten into his eye. Not yet catching on, I wondered what could have possibly flown into his eye to make it water so much. And then it struck me that Herr Diel, my brusque and formal instructor, the cracker of heads with his cane, had been moved to release at least one tear at the thought of my departure. It was momentous.

It took little encouragement from Herr Diel for me to travel promptly to the town of Forchheim to meet Edgar and Gertrude Klaus. For a young man starting out, I was duly impressed by their beautiful house, immaculate stables, and arena, all brand new. I would be in charge of six horses, and they were willing to buy more in the future. This was already a rather dazzling prospect, even before they showed me my own two-bedroom apartment, which came with the job—a luxury after Flensburg—as well as the offer of breakfast made by a neighbor (who wasn't Frau Wabbel) and dinner at a local inn. The icing on this astonishing cake was that, should I like to bring a horse, a free stall would be made available. It was an absolute dream job, and I quickly accepted.

When September arrived, I packed up the few belongings I had into a wicker trunk my mother had sent from Haderslev, and stowed them in my trusty red Beetle. It's funny how we can become sentimentally attached to objects in our lives, and because that wicker trunk accompanied me through much of my young adulthood, I've never been able to give it away—it's been like a quiet friend who shared in all those early experiences. Remarkably, it's even held together after all these years, and remains in my house to this day. At the time, in comparison, there was not much of a sentimental feeling as I bid farewell to Flensburg; even though I owed much to the place and to Herr Diel, I had been champing at the bit to begin my career and fly the coop. It was time. As I drove bemusedly along to Forchheim, which is a couple of hours north of Nuremberg, the reality of how rural it actually was struck me. I passed farmers driving hay wagons pulled by mules; and perched on top of these wagons were bouncing *hausfraus* whose ample bottoms secured the hay to keep it from flying away.

Herr Klaus, I learned, had started riding late in life. During the week, his factories took much of his time, and so he was only able to ride on the weekends. Frau Klaus was a careful rider who had a marvelous schoolmaster that had been trained by Harry Boldt, but was now in his 21st year and had retired from competition. Named Liostro, he was the first horse I rode after my arrival. Eager to show my new employers my capabilities as a rider, I asked my willing partner for several movements, particularly flying changes. Liostro could do the one tempis—flying changes every stride—and I must have ridden over a dozen.

It was delicious to ride such a beautifully trained horse, and I couldn't resist—I must have ridden something like 45 changes the following day, until I was approached tentatively by Frau Klaus, hands clasped before her, saying, "Herr Ostergaard, I'm afraid I must dampen your enthusiasm and ask you to please take into account that Liostro is an older horse who is no longer used to working so hard." Slightly chagrined, I nodded, but I will admit that I believed Liostro enjoyed it as much as I did, and when no one was around, I took the liberty of sneaking in a few flying changes here and there.

Perhaps to give a break to Liostro, Herr and Frau Klaus presented me with a wonderful opportunity: I traveled with them to the world-renowned horse auction in Verden, which is the center for breeding

Hanoverians, and there they purchased an impressive young mare named Sonatine. Before long, we were competing successfully, and Frau Klaus rode in one of these competitions, too.

At this particular competition, Frau Klaus was to ride a test in an area that was surrounded by heavily laden apple trees. In the middle of the free walk, on a long rein down the long side, Sonatine could no longer resist the heavenly aroma of the ripe fruit filling the air, and cunningly reached up to snatch an apple from a limb without a break in her stride. As any competitive rider can imagine, Frau Klaus was mortified, and her husband's remark, "At least it wasn't a banana," didn't help. The judges, however, only remarked in their scoring that the horse "showed fine movement in her neck and shoulders!"

In addition to my responsibility for the six horses owned by my employers, there were also multiple riders that came through the stable where I taught. I was busy, productive, and highly motivated. The only problem was that there were few people my age, and I was lacking any sort of social life. Herr and Frau Klaus sensed this, and in their generosity, they often included me on their trips and issued frequent invitations to dine together.

Yet Forchheim was a very small town, and the only other young people were guest workers from Turkey. As we didn't speak each other's language, there was little there to be gained. I even called upon the tedious dancing lessons of my youth and, nattily attired in coat and tie, thought perhaps I could meet a girl or two at the local dance class in town. One time was enough for me—it was a beginner's class, meaning we never even danced; the only instruction concerned the correct formal approach to asking a young lady to dance: striding purposefully toward a row of bored-looking girls, standing erect (did we click our heels together? I can't recall), and bowing slightly from the waist before making our request. Clearly I wouldn't be holding any buxom girls in dirndls in my arms that day, so I left and drove home, somewhat dispiritedly. I did, however, summon the courage to invite the innkeeper's daughter out to dinner in Nuremberg, and she actually did wear a dirndl. It was just one date; however, I will say that not only were the dishes of southern German cuisine appetizing, the view was, too.

May soon rolled around, and with it, softer, sunnier weather as well as my parents' 25th anniversary. They had decided against a big party, and, rather touchingly, chose to bring the closest members of the family to Germany and celebrate with me. My father had always been very fond of cars, and just as he had loved riding around town on our flashy, spotted Johnny, he loved riding in a nice car. In the mid-1960s, not everyone could afford a car. And certainly not the kind of car my father had.

If Herr Diel's Volkswagen was "the devil," my father's automobile could only be called "Godzilla." He had purchased a beast: a 1957 Ford Fairlane. This very large and very American car, with its white paint and red bumpers, threatened to devour any Volkswagen it drove behind. The vehicle had plenty of room for everyone, which probably could have included a billiard table and llama. My parents and my mother's brother sat in the front seat, while far behind in the back, in a separate zip code, sat her sister and both their spouses. In high spirits, they set off for Germany, without it occurring to anyone that if the car—being the only one of its kind in both Denmark and Germany—had broken down, spare parts would be impossible to obtain, and they would have had to spend their anniversary on the side of the road. But their journey was successful, and the car, with six people and six suitcases, arrived a few days before the big celebration.

I had been given the responsibility of planning both their stay and the party. I housed everyone at the inn in Burg Gaillenreuth. It felt good to be earning money, and with a certain sense of pride, I had spent a generous part of my paycheck buying a large silver platter, upon which I had had my parents' names engraved. I arranged for them to have their own suite with a balcony, which was typical of the traditional, half-timbered houses that are everywhere in Bavaria. Such a balcony was perfect for the Danish tradition of waking the bridal couple with horn music.

One of Herr Klaus's customers was the conductor of the local orchestra. I had asked whether they would consider "serenading" my parents that particular morning, and he was happy to oblige. The group turned up wearing their leather lederhosen and Tyrolean hats with feathers, and carrying their instruments, giving my parents a morning wake-up call they would never forget. Inexperienced as I was, I shook hands with the conductor to seal our agreement that there would be no fee as long as I paid for the beers the orchestra drank. I went along readily. After all, how much could that be, so early in the morning? It was a hard lesson, to learn that a Bavarian man can drink his weight in beer and a group of them can consume a silo of the stuff in one sitting. They drank beer like the rest of us drank water. Luckily for me, the innkeeper allowed me to pay off the tab over time. Still, it was a great day, with a brass "oom-pah-pah" band, festivities, and wonderful food. Later, I was relieved to hear that my family also managed to get back to Denmark in one piece, but shortly afterwards, Godzilla broke down and ended its colorful days at the scrap yard.

You might think me mad, and even ungrateful, when I say that, despite the generosity of Herr and Frau Klaus and the lovely horses I had at my disposal, I was beginning to feel restless. Bored. Forchheim was simply too far away from competitions and the horse industry in general. At 22, I was laser-focused on my career, and passionately hoping to become a professional rider and trainer. Remaining where I was felt as though I was spinning my wheels. It was time to move on.

CHAPTER
9

BACK HOME

WHILE IN RESIDENCE WITH THE KLAUS FAMILY, I had sub-scribed to a Danish paper, *Berlingske Tidende*, just to keep up with goings-on back home. The Sunday paper made it to my mailbox by each Wednesday, and I devoured it from front to back. In the "Sport" section, there was always a page devoted to news in the horse community: horses and farms for sale, competition results, and the occasional job offering. While perusing the paper one evening, I saw a job advertisement that practically had my name on it. The de-scription was of a position for a *bereiter* in a private stable rented from Frederiksdal Castle by a man named Torben Uhre. There was no school to run or board of directors to report to. Instead, I could choose my own clients. I got in touch at once.

The job interview was arranged, and the distance traveled would require taking a flight—I had never flown on a plane before, and looked forward to that. Torben offered to pay half of the cost of the ticket, per-haps to test my commitment, and I accepted. If I remember correctly, I mentioned to Herr and Frau Klaus that I needed to take a long week-end off, and I flew to Copenhagen, where Torben was waiting for me.

I assumed we'd be heading straight to Frederiksdal, but Torben had other ideas, and instead we made numerous stops at several rid-ing schools in the area. I had no idea why we were doing this, or why Torben was making such a point of asserting how much of a mess they were. "Look how poorly they've stacked that hay," he'd remark, as we pulled into one place. "Look how that fence needs repairing," he'd say about another.

It dawned on me as we pulled onto his street that this had been his way of telling me that he expected a certain standard to be maintained at his own stable. And, truth be told, it did not disappoint. Torben's stables overlooked the beautiful main building, surrounded by dense forest, with a glimmering view of Lake Furesø. Everything was immaculate. Slightly dazed, I followed him on a tour of the stable—cleaned, oiled bridles and saddles neatly hanging in place, aisles swept, horses gleaming.

Afterwards, he dropped me off at quite a nice hotel for which he had paid, and invited me to his home for dinner. In some ways, Torben reminded me of my father, in that he liked nice things and he liked his nice things to be noticed. When he suggested an after-dinner snifter of cognac, it was the first time I had ever witnessed what would later become the rage in all newly constructed, upscale houses of that era: a sunken living room.

Leaning back with confidence into his plushly upholstered chair, he took a swallow of cognac, looked me in the eye, and said, "I am happy to offer you the job." He was somewhat taken aback when I thanked him but replied that I would like to think about it. In all honesty, my mind was made up to accept it before I boarded the plane the following day.

During that conversation, he even offered me a free stall should I want to bring a horse, and requested I begin in August. I was over the moon. Now the only thing left was for me to inform the Klaus family.

This wasn't easy. They had been kind, hospitable, generous employers, and were understandably disappointed when I broke the news.

"I would have hoped you would stay at least a year," Herr Klaus allowed, and I couldn't blame him. And yet, when I spoke the truth—that as much as I had enjoyed working for them, I was lonely and missing Denmark—they relented and we parted amicably. In fact, they even visited me after I returned to my home country.

It was good to be back "home." Prior to this move, I had, during one of my outings with Krista, traveled to Copenhagen while I was still in Flensburg. It had been an impulsive trip for me, inspired by a letter I had written to the world-famous Danish trainer Gunnar Andersen during my first year with Herr Diel. I had been aware of his reputation from my early days with Johnny, especially as he had been the trainer of Lis Hartel, the first woman to win a medal in dressage at the 1952 Helsinki Olympics—and she did so despite having contracted debilitating polio. And it is no exaggeration to say that it was Andersen's students and horses that made up Danish teams for years. Call it a fan letter if you must, but at that time I was already thinking ahead about my future and working to establish contacts. And so I wrote to this distinguished top trainer in order to introduce myself, compliment his renowned ability, and express my hope to perhaps one day meet.

It was during 1967 that Krista and I took it upon ourselves to visit Gunnar Andersen at Havegaard. It seems audacious now that I had not called or written to say I was coming, especially since I had no idea whether he had ever read, or even received, my letter from years ago. And yet I was welcomed with open arms. He could not have been kinder. I am not stating anything that other riders wouldn't state: fame in the horse world is often accompanied by an oversized ego and a tendency to be self-absorbed. But with this man, nothing could be further from the truth. He listened attentively when I told him about my training in Germany and my plans to return to Denmark at some point. I was agog at the number of Grand Prix horses in his stable—the quality was outstanding—and I had the opportunity to watch him train several.

It was a wonderful visit, and at one point in our conversation, he wiggled the lash of a riding crop for a stable cat to paw and play with, a great smile on his face. As Krista commented drily on that moment, during our return journey, "Diel would never do such a thing!" And she was right. Two different trainers, two entirely different personalities. Had I never met Gunnar Andersen again, that meeting would still have remained powerfully memorable.

But just as with many things in my life, it was instead the beginning of yet another "full circle" story.

CHAPTER
10

MAISON DE PLAISANCE

As MOST PEOPLE OF MY VINTAGE REMEMBER, Neil Armstrong blasted off for the moon on July 16th, 1969. The day was hugely significant for me, as while my VW Beetle didn't exactly blast off, my dreams did, and I packed up all my belongings to head for Frederiksdal Castle in North Zealand. Everything that wouldn't fit went ahead by train, safely tucked inside my wicker trunk.

I had officially left my position in Forchheim on July 1st, and had planned to take a languid stretch of time to myself as a holiday before arriving at Torben's stable on August 1st. It was a convenient opportunity to visit both my parents and Krista in the three weeks that would follow, and would entail about a week's drive.

Driving along on that bright, warm summer's day, it felt as if a promising career was spreading out before me as, for the first time, I would be working for myself. While I was to keep an eye on the horses and lessons at Torben's stable, I could establish my own teaching and training business—an opportunity I relished.

From my car radio, I caught intermittent news updates about the progress of Apollo 11, and there was a powerful sentiment, both from the broadcasters and within my own Beetle, that there really was nothing humanity couldn't do. By the time I arrived at Krista's summer house, just outside Haderslev on Flovt Strand, Neil Armstrong, Michael Collins, and "Buzz" Armstrong had landed safely on the lunar surface, and, mesmerized, we watched Neil Armstrong's first legendary steps on the moon. That moment was, for me (and I can only assume for the entire planet), enormously significant. Filled with inspiration, I felt as if I were also on the cusp of stepping into an entirely new world—and the possibilities were endless. Two weeks later, this feeling continued to simmer within me as I turned into the parking area in front of the castle.

Downton Abbey it was not—in fact, it was more of a manor house, as opposed to boasting ostentatious turrets or any sort of fussy, gothic facade. Composed of elegant white masonry and topped with a black, hipped roof, Frederiksdal Castle is considered the earliest example of a *maison de plaisance* ("pleasure palace") in Denmark. And there was already a buzz in the air as it awaited the arrival of the new trainer.

A group of curious, expectant riding students—mostly teenage girls—loitered around the long, low-ceilinged stables, which had been converted from the original farm buildings, hoping to get a glimpse. I can't say whether I lived up to their expectations or not...

However, I was more interested in making a solid impression with my training abilities, and that came quickly. One of my first students, who was like a stepdaughter to Torben, was Astrid Hendrup. She owned a mare named Kassandra, who stood in the very first stall on the right. This horse was not exactly built for the sport: she had a bit of a hay belly, balanced on four coffee table legs, and "Asser," as Astrid was known, informed me that the mare was incapable of lengthening her trot. Astrid had accepted this disappointment as fact because the prior trainer—who specialized in show jumping and not dressage—had told her the mare simply didn't have the ability. It immediately occurred to me that if I could achieve an extended trot on Kassandra, I would be regarded with respect straight away. It didn't happen overnight—but Kassandra and I schooled doggedly for the next three weeks, until the mare engaged her hind end and loosened her shoulders, which not only transformed her movement before the "rail birds" who watched our sessions, but also sent Astrid and Kassandra up the levels rapidly. They competed flourishingly up to 4th Level. It was exactly the start I had hoped for.

Word of this "new trainer" spread quickly, and more people came for lessons. While at first it may have been to satisfy their curiosity, these students returned for further lessons. My motivation resulted in a schedule filled with lessons, horses in training, and commissions from the riding school. I began to relax a little. The rigid formality of Germany, which had really defined me both as a rider and young man, had followed me with an air of strict, no-nonsense discipline and attention to detail. The problem was that it had followed me to a country which considered it a bit much.

Although Denmark and Germany share a border, I have experienced the difference between the countries first-hand. It was like night and day. The counterculture of 1960s America had been enthusiastically embraced by Danish youth, with jeans and T-shirts adding to the already entrenched casual nature of the Danes. Technically, Danish and German both have a formal and informal way to say "you," but in Denmark, the formal "you" was already growing rare, even back then; in Germany, all adults were addressed with the formal "you," and only children and friends were addressed by their names. In Flensburg, I had grown up under Herr Diel's expert guidance, and had been exposed to people who had known each other for many years before asking if they could address each other by their first names. And so while Denmark was my homeland, it would take me some time to shed this layer of formality that now felt so natural to me—beginning on that first day, as I agonized over how to address Astrid. Upon first meeting her, I had no idea whether I should address her by her first name, or call her Mrs. Hendrup—to even consider using her nickname Asser seemed unthinkable. In the end, I avoided calling her anything for days, until I observed everyone calling everyone else by their first names.

The need to loosen up further became apparent when I contacted my cousin Kirsten, who lived in Copenhagen. The time I had spent with the Klaus family had inspired me to establish friendships with people outside the horse world. Kirsten was glad to hear from me, and I was promptly invited to a party. Not thinking twice, I dressed as was my long-established habit for any non-equestrian outing: white shirt, jacket, and tie. Stepping inside, I was greeted by the sight of everyone else wearing jeans and tie-dyed T-shirts; I must have looked like an accountant arriving to assist the party-goers with their taxes. Mortified, I stepped quickly back outside, pulled off my tie and jacket, and unbuttoned my shirt. Lesson learned, I thought, as the mood lightened considerably.

I'd like to say that I'm a quick learner. I'd like to say that, but it has not always been the case, and this was evident a few weeks later, when a group of us decided to go to the theater to see a play. While living in Flensburg, my friend Nis Valdemar took me to see "The Merry Widow," as well as other performances, and we always wore our dark blue suits, looking indistinguishable from every other guest in attendance. It was simply normal to dress respectably for a night out, and never in my wildest dreams could I imagine anyone would even consider showing up at a theater in jeans and a T-shirt. But in Denmark, they did! So once again, I had to duck out the door and change my appearance so as not to stick out like a sore thumb in a sea of Levis, shaggy hair, and the pervasive scent of patchouli. My dark navy suit, evidently only appropriate for funerals, never again saw the light of day, and hung, banished, in the back of my closet.

CHAPTER
11

HALCYON DAYS

THE FIRST CHALLENGE FOR ME upon moving back to Denmark, was, oddly enough, finding a place to live and actually remaining there. To explain: when I first arrived in Frederiksdal, Torben had arranged for me to sublet an apartment in Virum. It had been a case of perfect timing; the primary occupant would be leaving to move in with her boyfriend. Everything seemed to be going to plan, until I arrived with all my belongings and found a note from her saying things "weren't working out with [her] boyfriend after all," meaning I was going to have to find another place to live—and quick.

I mentioned in the last chapter the casual attitude that prevails in Denmark, as opposed to Germany, and perhaps for the next landlord, there had been a bit too much of that attitude, as the next place I found—an available room in nearby Holte—was crossed off the list after the old man's first question was whether or not I had syphilis! I left skid marks, I think, leaving that place. I finally found a room in Virum that I could rent from one of Torben's neighbors, but it wasn't ideal. All of this apartment-hopping was becoming a bit frustrating. Here I was, training out of the stables of a castle, and having difficulty finding a decent place to live. Enter Jane Malmkjaer, who became a great friend and remains so to this day. Jane kept her horse stabled at Frederiksdal, and she lived with her mother in quite a large house nearby. They had the extra room, and so I was invited to move in.

Jane, her husband, and their five children have all visited us in the United States. Three of her children have even worked for us. The oldest girl loved horses while the boys didn't care for them as much, but together, we collected stones from every corner of the property that were ultimately used for the exterior walls of our house in Vermont—gathering them in the fields, along the creek, and into the woods—which means they are part of some of the happiest memories Birgit and I have. We still visit each other in Denmark and in the United States.

At any rate, back then, with a consistent address at last, and a string of students and horses to train, I was beginning to settle comfortably into my life at Frederiksdal. I felt content and confident in my ability, as all the horses in my training were developing according to my expectations. The apple of my eye was Lotus, a Hanoverian mare imported from Germany. In those days, that was pretty impressive, as it was quite expensive to import horses from Germany. She was a beautiful mare who moved well enough to be competitive in dressage and had the bonus ability of being able to jump.

With happy anticipation, I entered Lotus in my first show since arriving back in Denmark. To be honest, I felt a little cocky. After all, I had been trained in Germany, was doing well in Denmark, and had a talented horse. Convinced that I would top the other competitors, I rode what I thought was a very good, error-free test, and left the arena with a smile on my face and a pat for the mare's neck.

When the score sheet was posted, I was gutted. I'd finished third, and at the bottom of the sheet the judges had written, "The rider is sitting crooked on the horse." How could that possibly be? How could I have not felt that? I was mortified, and wished the ground beneath my feet would open up and swallow me whole. It is said that pride goeth before a fall, and it certainly did with me. That day, I wasn't just served a slice of humble pie, I was given the whole thing.

My self-esteem in tatters, I wandered around the showgrounds to watch the other classes. I had heard of a show-jumping trainer named N.K. Hansen, who had an envious string of wealthy clients, good horses, and skilled riders. I spotted Hansen riding a horse that was notorious for refusing, but with N.K. in the saddle, that was not an option for this horse. It was rumored that he sometimes trained wearing two pairs of spurs—which says something about his style. As I watched him soar over jump after jump, I couldn't have known that at the time one of his clients was my future wife—but it would be several years before I met her.

One of the things that was becoming apparent in Denmark was that I was expected to be able to teach show jumping as well as dressage. I had jumped, and even competed in jumping—it had been required in order to earn my *bereiter* certificate—but my focus in Flensburg had been dressage. In Denmark, however, that wasn't the way it was done. You both jumped and rode dressage.

There was only one thing to do: find a book on the subject; memorize the details such as distances and combinations, as well as teaching methods; and then try to sound as if I knew what the hell I was talking about. In the end, I did absorb the material, and actually sounded quite convincing.

While my students weren't on the road to becoming professional show jumpers, they indeed improved, and our lessons went well. Luckily, these students only jumped once a week, and the indoor riding hall wasn't nearly big enough for advanced jumping!

I enjoyed adding more jumping to my own personal repertoire, even if I didn't always come home with a ribbon. Lotus, with her abilities in both dressage and jumping, also possessed the frustrating ability to regularly drop a rail somewhere on the course, thus earning four faults at competitions.

Sergeant was another horse in the stable with whom I tackled some courses. He actually started out very well. But as the jumps got higher, his courage dropped like a stone. It always happened at the last possible second: he would decide he'd had enough and would slam on the brakes. If nothing else, he strengthened my ability to stay in the saddle.

I finally found success on a Thoroughbred cross named Tonka, who had courage in spades. He was fearless. His owner was a bit "over-mounted," and found Tonka somewhat intimidating, which gave me the opportunity to take the horse to a few shows. The one I will never forget was at one of the more impressive venues in North Zealand—the place to be in Denmark, if you wanted to seriously pursue the horse industry—and this competition was for professionals only.

In this particular class, N.K. Hansen and I were the last two left in the jump-off, and it seemed we were going to end up with a tied result, as the rails had been raised to the highest point possible on the jump standards. And then some genius had the idea to place beer crates under the standards to raise them even higher. Impossible, to-day, to think that anyone would even dream of allowing such a thing, but perhaps the beer in the crates had all been consumed at the show, so no one cared. In the end—and I still can't believe it—Tonka and I cleared the triple bar at 6' 4" (1.95 meters). It was the first and last time I would jump that high in my life.

Things felt as though they were beginning to snowball in a very good way for me, upon moving back to Denmark. Two events would go on to have a profound effect on my life and career. The first was meeting Ellen Holm, an American who had married in Denmark and was fluent in the language. She was married to the president of the Danish Breeding Society, and knew everyone. This was because she was the type of person who wouldn't hesitate to reach out and welcome any new trainer on the scene. That was her way, and she remained wonderfully warm and inclusive until her death at age 92.

Ellen reached out to me and I liked her immediately. She was both curious about and interested in my training, from Denmark to Germany, and we got to know each other quite well. With her help, I established my first contact with Linda Zang, who brought an older Swedish gentleman, "Reitmaster Bonnesen," to watch me ride. Standing stiffly beside the rail and sternly appraising my ability, he made a comment about me that day which later became a running joke between Ellen and I: "This man is a good rider, if he will learn to look up!" Often after that, when I would see her glancing my way, even if I had just pulled into the parking lot with my car, I would comedically stretch my neck and jerk up my chin. We shared a lot of laughs over that.

The other life-changing event was reacquainting myself with Gunnar Andersen. I had had no contact with him since my original visit two years ago, but I contacted him fairly soon after I arrived at Frederiksdal. We agreed that Wednesday would suit us both, and so I made the half-hour drive to his stable, and found him as affable and approachable as I had remembered.

His laugh was contagious—so much so, I was told, that as a young boy, his friends would give him free tickets to the cinema if he would simply laugh for them. That first Wednesday turned into a weekly visit, and I truly felt from the beginning that he was taking a special interest, and even putting me on his Grand Prix horses, which was heaven on earth. This man, the face of Danish dressage for forty years, seemed to have taken it upon himself to become my mentor.

Gunnar seemingly had no ego; whether that was because he had been brought up by a father who had had a lower-level career in the Army, I don't know, but he remained both humble and respectful all the years I knew him. It was never about money with Gunnar Andersen—he had no desire to become a businessman, he simply lived his passion day after day, and he was particularly keen on producing hot-blooded Thoroughbreds. While European Warmbloods were making their mark on the competition scene, particularly in Germany, Gunnar remained faithful to his Thoroughbreds, and said that in order to bring home a ribbon, they had to be "twice as good to beat the Germans." And many were. His list of Thoroughbreds that made the Danish Team was long: Atmospherics, Inferno, Souliman, and the very talented C'est Bon.

When the Danish Warmblood Talisman came into his stable, he trained the horse to a place on the Danish team for the 1972 Munich Games, with Aksel Mikkelsen in the saddle. While the team just missed out on a medal, it was Talisman's score, finishing a respectable 11th out of a field of 35, that brought the Danish team within striking distance of a bronze. The commentators and sport journalists of the day were quick to point out that Talisman had the best piaffe of any horse in the class.

I lived for Wednesdays—I couldn't get enough. But one Wednesday was particularly memorable. There had been a terrific snowstorm, and I had doggedly crawled along the road in my intrepid Beetle. I nearly turned around three times, as the snow was above the hubcaps and the wipers were doing little to keep the flakes from gathering and freezing across the windshield. When I finally limped into the parking area, I got out of my car, trudged through the snow, and—I'll never forget it—shoved open the massive barn door, blinking as my eyes adjusted from the blinding snow to the low light of the indoor arena. Before me was Gunnar, puffing away on the pipe habitually in his mouth and performing the most exquisite piaffe I had ever seen on Talisman. The gleaming white of Talisman's coat, as bright as the snow that had swirled around me outside, was filigreed by the morning light now streaming in...It was like watching a movie: horse and rider framed in the doorway, moving from piaffe into passage and back into piaffe—classically correct and utterly breathtaking. With his trademark droll humor, he glanced over at me and remarked nonchalantly, "Huh, didn't think you'd make it."

That this man would take me beneath his wing and give me the opportunity to ride all those horses...horses that he had trained and competed with renowned success. Gunnar was unbelievably generous with his knowledge, and never made a big deal out of handing me the reins of one of these international Grand Prix horses and saying, as if offering a little kid a pony ride at a fair, "Here, you can try a ride on this one."

These were halcyon days. I was receiving training I could have only dreamt about with Gunnar, establishing a steady business for myself, and developing a social life with friends my own age. As winter thawed into spring, then summer, I was amused, if also somewhat taken aback, by the casual Danish attitude spilling over into the stable with the arrival of July.

As in Germany, Danish horses were never turned out. They lived in their stalls, and were ridden and then put back into their stalls. Except, that is, for one month in Denmark, when the majority of the population took their summer vacation and caution was thrown to the wind.

Beginning July 1st, the barn would close down and, astonishingly, every horse in the barn, whether privately owned or a school horse, was turned out, banding together as a herd in a 20-acre field. I couldn't believe it: no protective boots, no concern for too much grass, no fly spray. But this was the way it had been done for fifty years. After the month was up, the horses were brought in and any scrapes or swellings would then be treated. I do not, however, recall any serious injury—I still shake my head over it.

After the horses had had a month to let their hair down, so did I, attending outings and parties thrown by friends. I will admit that some days my head felt a bit fresher than others; still, I was in the saddle of the first horse every morning by seven o'clock, and I loved it.

CHAPTER
12

STEPPING STONES

A N EARLY "CLAIM TO FAME" came into my life with the arrival of a gray gelding named Losiac. He was owned by a young woman who had no interest in competitive riding; she had bought the horse from his breeder as a four-year-old, and gave me the ride. Having Losiac in my stable for three years was one of my first opportunities to produce a horse up to Prix St. Georges, and I learned a lot from that process—even today, I use the same methodology when training other horses. With Losiac, I won the huge 4th-level National Open class at Holte. This was the first show in which classes were no longer divided between amateurs and professionals, but combined together, and it was a pretty big deal. The score sheets hadn't been put up when I left to stop by yet another rider's party after the show, and it was only when I checked in that I was told I'd won this preeminent class. So instead of "stopping by," I stayed with the others, partying until the wee hours. It was unbelievable that people could drink until four in the morning and then be on their horses, warming up, at seven o'clock. Ah, youth!

It was a feather in my cap when Losiac was later sold to a rider who continued to develop him up to Grand Prix. I won't tell you the price, even in today's dollars, but Losiac's subsequent sale at that time made him the most expensive horse registered by the Danish Sport Horse Breeders' Association. And I will tell you that it was around what someone might pay for a used Kia hatchback. A used Kia hatchback with a ding in the driver's door. This was during the 1970s, the early years of the Danish Warmblood. Yet that sale was an eye-popping price in those days, and I was proud of my part in it.

The other Prix St Georges horse I produced was with one of my advanced students, my good friend Ina Zetterstrom—a funny, effervescent girl who, for years, was always the one to bring all the Frederiksdal riders back together for parties. Ina had a large Connemara pony mare named Miniwyn that had been going at 4th level. Ina was a competent enough rider that I gave her the ride on Gaston, at 3rd level.

Gaston was a horse that had come to me through the influence of Ellen Holm, who dropped by in 1971 to say she'd seen a nice Trakehner youngster; following her lead, I went to see him. Gaston, as I later renamed him, didn't blow me away, but he was big, black, and had a great hind leg. I thought I could do something with him, and wrote the check. He did, however, come very set in the jaw, which made training a bit difficult. Yet Gaston went on to win a large 3rd level class at Herning with Ina in the saddle, racked up a lot of wins at 4th level, and was about to debut at Prix St Georges when tragedy struck. Turned out in his paddock, Gaston leapt over the fence and cleared it, but landed on his knees, injuring himself so badly he had to be euthanized.

Work was steadily increasing, with more and more demand for lessons and training. After a year at Frederiksdal, I decided I could be more productive if I had a bit of help with the running of the stable. The perfect solution was a young man named Erik Agner Nielsen.

Erik was someone who wanted to work with horses but didn't want to compete or train as a riding student. With Erik on board to oversee the care of the horses, I could focus solely on training and teaching. Erik had a great sense of humor; the two of us clicked well and had a lot of fun. We were also not adverse to playing the occasional practical joke, and another acquaintance, Gert Poulsen, was the focus of a prank that still makes me laugh.

Gert was a lovely man in his 60s who stabled his black mare, Nike, with us. Having no competitive aspirations, Gert was what today might be called a "happy hacker," who simply enjoyed riding his imported Polish mount around the glorious countryside surrounding the estate.

Nike was named not after a tennis shoe, but after the winged Greek goddess of victory in all things artistic, including athletics. After watching this mare trot along like a sewing machine, I could only suspect there had been a great spirit of optimism when she was born and named. Nike was, however, oddly comfortable to sit, and this was an advantage for her not-so-experienced rider.

Erik owned a horse that was also black, but that was where the similarities ended. Unlike Nike, Erik's mount was decidedly part cart-horse in his lineage: big, clunky, with the kind of knee action that would help pull a plow through a muddy field.

Between us, we cooked up the outrageous idea of swapping horses for Gert, and when the gentleman showed up punctually for his usual eight-o'clock ride, one particularly dark winter morning, he found "his" horse, as usual, tacked up and waiting. It was all Erik and I could do to keep our faces straight as we incredulously watched Gert mount "Nike" and set off for the riding hall. He didn't notice the difference in the horse's height or conformation, and, unbelievably, rode around the hall three times before he realized something was wrong. Pulling Erik's gelding to a halt, he roared, "Ostergaard! What the hell is wrong with my horse?" At that point, Erik and I burst out laughing. Thankfully, Gert saw the humor in it, too, and laughed as well.

These were happy times that were also filled to the brim with hard work, each and every day. With the passing of another year, I was in a position to hire another employee—this time, an assistant trainer.

As luck would have it, a young man named Jorgen Olsen, who had just finished his riding degree in Sweden, accepted my offer to assist me with teaching and riding the horses. He had a great work ethic, rode with me for a year, and then took a job at a riding club in North Zealand. His abilities led him to ride and compete at Grand Prix, but his forte was his superb eye for a horse. Indeed, it was Jorgen who bought the young stallion Rambo, and got him approved as a stallion—no small feat in Denmark. He trained the horse to Grand Prix, then sold him to Richard Freeman, where Heather Blitz took over the ride. And I myself have bought several great horses from Jorgen over the years, too.

The only fly in the ointment during that time was the task of bookkeeping. Because I had an employee, I was obliged not only to pay wages, but keep up with all the paperwork required to report to the tax authorities. This meant I had to keep two separate accounts: one for personal use and one for business, which included having to track every mile I drove. This relentless bureaucracy with its stacks of paperwork kept me an unwilling captive at my desk when I needed to be riding. Even then, I remember thinking, "There must be an easier way." And while I did fortunately have a relative in Copenhagen who could help me get it all done properly, my brain was beginning to flit toward conversations I had had with Ellen Holm.

During one of our chats, Ellen had told me about her family's farm in Annapolis, Maryland. Having been enamored with the United States since I was a boy, I had asked her several questions about both the horses and the lifestyle "over there." I was careful, however, not to reveal the dream that was beginning to manifest itself within me. As successful as I was becoming at Frederiksdal, I had always considered it a stepping stone toward something much bigger.

And America was beginning to loom large in my mind.

CHAPTER
13

THE WHOLE PACKAGE

ANYONE WHO WAS ANYONE in the Danish horse world attended the big annual March show at the Sports Riding Club in Gentofte, just north of Copenhagen. All the respected dressage and show-jumping riders would compete, and the venue was considered top-notch and state-of-the-art because it was the only facility around that offered two riding halls: one for warming up and one for the actual competition. And, funnily enough, the "big" arena back then was the size of today's small arena, measuring just 20 by 40 meters!

For me, it was yet another "full-circle" experience. I had first come to Gentofte in 1967, a bit goggle-eyed, as a groom for a client's horse while I was still an apprentice at Flensburg. Yet here I was, six years later, head trainer at Frederiksdal, with a string of horses competing.

As was the norm, I was also show jumping, and as I got on my horse and headed out to warm up, I caught sight of a beautiful young woman, her dark hair swept back in a ponytail, tracking left on a loose rein at the walk. I'd spotted Birgit Helt-Hansen at other shows—everyone knew of her—but I had never had the opportunity, or, frankly, the nerve, to approach this up-and-coming celebrity.

Birgit had been trained by N.K. Hansen, who was the jumping trainer in Denmark, and she had racked up multiple wins as a rider in team competition for the Hesselrød Riding Club. Those successes led to her being featured in various riding magazines. But it was her laser-like focus and dedication to both her horses and training that earned her the respect of everyone in the Danish equine world.

Birgit had fixed up an older stable not far from where she lived, north of Copenhagen, and besides doing the feeding and mucking, somehow managed to squeeze in riding a couple of horses very early each morning before she left for work—a full-time position as a lab technician—and then rode her other horses after work. The only time she had outside help was during her workdays, when she had someone throw the horses hay at lunch and top up their water buckets. And while Birgit had access to an indoor riding hall, it was about half a mile away—which meant that during the endless short days and long nights of the fall and winter, she was making her way on horseback to and from the hall in the dark, regardless of the weather. Her dogged determination paid off: she was competing in both Denmark and Sweden at the highest level, and winning.

It's interesting, the clarity that comes with memories of life-changing events. I can vividly recall that we were both walking on the left rein, and that attached to the lapel of her beautifully fitted black jacket, she had a small, colorful insignia. In my short life, I had fallen in love a few times—that topsy-turvy, all-encompassing passion that comes with youth and brings no lasting commitment. And yet, the moment I laid eyes on Birgit, before we even spoke, I knew this was someone different. She was lovely, she had a work ethic I understood, and as an up-and-coming rider myself, I admired her success. She was, to put it plainly, the whole package. And even more plainly, I was mesmerized enough to chat her up.

Quiet, yet approachable, Birgit returned my hello and we spoke for a little while as I rode up alongside her. She spoke softly, and when she smiled, so did her large and expressive eyes. Breaking away to loosen up her horse and begin his warm-up, she bid me adieu. Relieved to have made a small in-road, I was smitten. Another student of N.K. Hansen, Annette Horsten, later remarked to Birgit, "I think that guy Ostergaard likes you." And I can say "that guy" was certainly pleased when N.K. Hansen—undoubtedly also informed of my attention to Birgit—invited me to a rider's party being thrown that night.

The gathering was held at Hesselrød. I made what I considered to be a subtle beeline for Birgit, and asked her to dance. As we moved around the dance floor, I don't know where it came from, but I had the audacity to say, "You should know I'm not exactly an easy person to deal with." Birgit said nothing in reply to that, but it's clear she tucked it away on a back burner in her brain, because over the course of a long and happy marriage, she has reminded me of my own words that night when needed!

Eager to see more of her, I then asked her (as only a horseman would) if she'd like to come see the jumpers I had in training at my stable, followed by a meal out. Because of her crowded schedule, Birgit would only be available to come over during the evening. Hoping to impress her, I arranged my own full schedule to save the best jumpers I had for last. The top of the heap was a big liver chestnut named Karaman, a gelding with huge scope. I had deliberately set up an imposing triple bar, placing the rails at the top of the standards.

Karaman soared over it, and, feeling pretty full of myself, I half-smiled as I dragged the jumps back out of the arena. Then Birgit (as only a horsewoman would) followed me back to my apartment so I could clean up before we headed out to dinner. How well I remember popping my head through the doorway, towel over my shoulder, before heading downstairs to shower, and saying, "Didn't that horse jump well?"

And Birgit, never looking up from the magazine she was flicking through, and probably with my "I'm not easy to deal with" declaration fresh in her mind, took me down a peg by replying, "Yes, but then you were easy on him, weren't you?" Meaning, I had set up a stretching triple for him instead of a more demanding vertical hurdle.

Her words served as a bit of an unexpected half-halt. I was unsettled by it, and the comment followed me as I went down to take my shower. Other girls I had known had been smilingly complimentary, eager to please. It was quite evident that Birgit was not like the others. And that was a good thing. Birgit was—and is—her own person, practical, capable, and honest. Rock solid, with no drama. I had felt keen respect for her before I even had the chance to meet her. That was a first for me. Suffice it to say I had never met anyone like her, and I was hooked.

I had chosen a trendy new restaurant (and definitely not chosen my accountant attire), determined to make a better impression. What I hadn't realized until we were inside was that it was a pizzeria—something quite new in Copenhagen, so not exactly a Pizza Hut. After a few moments standing about, feeling rather awkward, Birgit shrugged her shoulders and said, "Why not? Let's give it a try." Part of me wondered whether that same sentiment applied to me, as this marked the first evening that we began to see each other exclusively.

It was quite something to have someone so dedicated and focused in my life, and we weaved together a relationship that incorporated our riding and competition schedules around the little free time that we had. In fact, I will admit to a bit of frustration as, while I was on my first horse of the day at seven o'clock, I was usually finished by five or six o'clock in the evening—whereas Birgit, going from her job as a lab technician to the stable, often wasn't finished until eight or nine at night. We did, however, manage to carve out time for ourselves.

This was actually a little easier to do at a show, and I remember going out to dinner after a competition to celebrate particularly good results. On a high, I mentioned that if I trained more horses for the Prix St Georges, then I would have reached my goal. Birgit looked at me for a moment and then stated, matter-of-factly, "You should train Grand Prix horses." This was Birgit in a nutshell. She had the courage to set big goals, and the tenacity to achieve them. Her attitude both inspired me and led her to become the Danish Grand Prix Show Jumping Champion in 1973.

That victory led to much notice, and even more press. I was actually driving when the news broke on my car radio that "Birgit Helt-Hansen has just won the Danish Grand Prix Show Jumping Championship." The local press was spot-on with the headline: "Diligent Girl Wins Championship." What many didn't realize is that she won with a late entry—beating the entire elite sweep of Danish riders. Decades later, we ran into one of the most successful show jumpers in Denmark, Per Siesby, who remembered the event well and commented drily, "That was very naughtily won."

As our relationship developed and became more serious, Birgit invited me to the home of her parents, Rita and Thorkild Helt-Hansen, for Easter dinner. At the time, I had a large and very enthusiastic golden retriever named Bodo, and despite the fact that her parents lived in an apartment, Birgit assured me it would be "just fine" for me to bring my dog with me on this first visit to my future in-laws, perhaps as a sort of furry ice-breaker. While Bodo didn't actually break any ice, he knocked over everything within his reach, and what he didn't knock over with his boisterous body, he swept down with his tail: wine glasses, coasters, a vase. To make matters worse, I topped off lunch by kiddingly complimenting the hostess on her superbly marinated homemade *heering* (herring) by enthusing, "Rita, these taste almost as good as the ones I buy in a can!" For a moment, considering the blank look on her face, I thought perhaps my joke had flown over her head, but alas, it had hit her right between the eyes, and she simply gaped. Birgit attempted to remedy the situation by explaining that my Southern Jutland sense of humor was a bit different than that of city dwellers in Copenhagen. Luckily, after brushing dog hair off my pants, the tablecloth, and the sofa, I had several other opportunities to get to spend time with my future in-laws, and we got along splendidly—although I never heard the end of that *heering* joke for as long as they lived.

By late 1973, months after our first meeting, Birgit and I had begun to share our horses as well. She had a Swedish Warmblood named Dorus, bred in Denmark with jumping bloodlines. Sometimes breeding doesn't matter, and in this case, it didn't, as Dorus showed no talent for fences. Birgit had backed him herself, riding him first in a small paddock, and then, as soon as he accepted her weight and carried her around, taking him half a mile down the country lane back to the barn. She was fearless, although I did help her at night as she rode down that dark road to the indoor arena.

When Dorus turned six and I was introducing him to flying changes, we hit a stumbling block and I couldn't get them consistent. My mentor Gunnar Andersen would then come over—it was quite the talk of the barn whenever he would show up—and climb aboard Dorus, quickly diagnosing the issue as straightness, which was something I never forgot. Those whom I train even today will hear me stress why straightness is vital.

As soon as Dorus learned his flying changes, he soared up the levels, and by age eight, he was competing in the Intermediare I. Prior to this, in November of 1975, the Danish Riding Instructors' Association was celebrating the 10th anniversary of its inception, and it was decided that a huge show would be held to mark the occasion. The venue was the Holte Riding Club, and, miracle of miracles, there was not only a 20 by 40-meter warm-up arena (imagine warming up in that with twenty other riders), but a competition arena, which was a full 20 by 60 meters. Spectators poured in, and it was quite the event.

I had entered the Prix St Georges Derby class, in which its 18 entrants were required to ride the test, and then the top four would be qualified for a ride-off. And in true "derby" style, the four of us changed horses three times, with a couple of minutes to get to know our new mounts before we rode a test. The winner would be the rider who scored the best initial test, combined with the best score given on the other three horses. Dorus was not the easiest horse to ride for the other riders, and as it turned out, it was my day. I won, and there is a funny photo of a sea of my students and clients hoisting me up on their shoulders and carrying me away in victory. It was a huge win for me, and attracted a lot of notice.

I continued to work all the hours God sent, and yet at the end of the week, it never seemed to be enough. I remember the defeated feeling I had after a few years at Frederiksdal, when I realized that I wouldn't be buying a home of my own anytime in the near future. I couldn't work any harder than I was. The truth of the matter was that I was being eaten alive by taxes, and it felt impossible to get ahead. I don't exaggerate when I say that Denmark has some of the highest—if not the highest—tax rates in the world. And anyone who competes horses knows first-hand how expensive that endeavor is, with the transportation, hotels, and meals. But as a professional trainer, it was necessary to be seen and do well at the shows.

While today, Birgit and I still have the beautiful, velvet-lined rosewood box of silver cutlery I won all those years ago, the other silver we won between us didn't buy oats or pay for the farrier. I can't remember whose idea it was, so I'll pin it on Birgit (because she's in the other room while I type) by saying she contrived a cunning scheme to take any silver punch bowls or serving trays we had been awarded to the local up-market department store in Copenhagen, which was called Magasin—the Danish version of Macy's. With her large, innocent eyes, she would explain ruefully that she had been given the silver as a wedding gift and therefore had no receipt, but as she didn't need the silver, could she have the money instead? No, she would be told by a clerk, but, inevitably, the clerk added that Birgit could exchange the silver for something else, and with that exchange, she would be given the needed receipt to be given the cash next time around. It was a brilliant ploy, and we would make a day of it, going into town and taking turns working as a team to enter the store shamelessly with our little white—or rather silver—lie.

CHAPTER
14

RIDE OUT OF TOWN!

A S MUCH AS I LOVED DENMARK, as much as it makes up my roots, I couldn't deny feeling increasingly claustrophobic. Blame it on the endless bureaucracy, runaway taxes, wanderlust, or Walter Farley; whatever the cause, I was not unlike a young horse desperate to be turned out into the field he knew was outside his stall. I had gotten my hands on an American horse magazine, and inside I found the names of two trainers that I contacted to see if they might be willing to help me find a job. They didn't reply, but dipping my toe into the potential job market overseas did give me the courage to share my dream—continuing my career in yet a third country: the United States—with Ellen.

The most obvious contact was one Ellen had introduced me to earlier: Linda Zang. She had seen me ride that day at Frederiksdal and remembered me well, and when Ellen phoned her on my behalf, I had a keen sense of déjà vu. Suddenly I was transported back to that moment when I was a young lad, sitting next to dear Frau Frerks as she phoned Herr Diel for me. And that same sense of excited anticipation began to simmer when Linda invited me to teach at her farm for three weeks during the summer of 1975.

Linda was one of the first people in the United States to import European dressage horses into the country. These days, no one thinks twice about importing or exporting a horse anywhere in the world by air. But back then, archaic as it sounds, horses crossed the Atlantic by ship. She had made the trip herself with the aptly named Fellow Traveller, in much the same way that I had traveled with my circus horse, Rhenus, to Norway many years earlier. Her stable was filled with Swedish horses, and one could easily suspect her relationship with Ellen Holm had a lot to do with that. In fact, on a somewhat funny note, Ellen, upon divorcing her husband Ole, snuck her horses off their farm and tried to fly them to the States.

However, this plan was thwarted when the flight was canceled, and she had to hustle like crazy to get them back to the farm. The scheme was rescheduled, and in late spring, the horses were snuck out once more, loaded onto a plane, and flown to New York. So unusual was it to see a horse on a plane that Ellen later told me a member of the ground crew at JFK looked with disgust at the soiled containment area in the plane, and remarked in pure Bronx dialect, "This looks like an effing farm!"

Linda and I had agreed that Birgit would be joining me, and it had been arranged that we would be staying at the home of Linda's parents. Our plans had been set into motion—everyone at Frederiksdal knew we were going, but they believed it was simply a vacation, since it was happening in July. As with the horses who were being turned out in the field for a month, I was finally getting turned out as well. With great excitement, for the second time in my life, I boarded a plane and was off.

This flight, unlike my first jaunt to Copenhagen, seemingly lasted forever, yet was thankfully uneventful. We did, however, arrive late, and missed the connection to Washington, D.C. The airline then announced over the speaker system that we stranded passengers would be herded onto a bus and driven to our final destination. The sheer size of the place, its swarming crowds, and the manic pace of JFK Airport had completely overwhelmed me, and although I rushed to get my money converted to American currency, I was struggling with my suitcase and legal documents, and had these brand-new coins mixed up with Danish kroner in my pocket. This led to frustration on the part of the bus driver; I, with my limited English, thought he was growling, "Goat change. Goat change!" Actually, he was ordering me to, "Get change!" with no livestock involved. Chastened, realizing I was holding up the line, I then experienced my first taste of American kindness. A complete stranger—a guy standing near me—stepped up and generously paid my fare out of his own pocket. I was unbelievably grateful and, with relief, took my seat.

It wasn't much better for Linda, who had to wait a full three hours at the bus terminal until I finally arrived. We then walked to her car, where I had a further one-hour journey to her family's Idlewilde Farm in Maryland. My body clock was chiming at 4:00 a.m., I was running on adrenaline, and when I followed Linda into the house and she offered me a beer, I asked earnestly, "Are you going to show me the horses?"

She looked at me blankly for a beat before replying, "Gunnar, it's 10 o'clock at night. I'm going to bed."

I was too keyed up to go to sleep and, taking my beer, I sat down and turned on the television to sample a bit of American culture. It was nothing but commercials! This was a shock to the system, and later on, with the exception of catching a few episodes of *All in the Family,* I rarely turned it on. Nothing was worth sitting through ten minutes of ads for Old Spice deodorant and pantyhose that came in big plastic eggs.

The following morning, I was up before dawn and eager to start work and experience my first impressions of Idlewilde. It didn't take long; I opened the door and was hit in the face by what felt to me like a blast furnace: the heat and humidity of a Maryland summer was un-like anything I'd ever felt. I wasn't even halfway to the stables when I could feel perspiration beading on my forehead and trickling down my neck. Each day felt as if I were wearing a hot, wet blanket. Definite-ly not the climate I was used to!

I had been told Bengt Ljungquist, the Swedish Olympian and later coach of the U.S. Pan Am and Olympic Teams, had been in the area teaching Linda, but for the time I remained, I honored our con-tract by fulfilling all work requirements. I taught Linda daily on Fel-low Traveller, the horse she would later take to the Pan Am Games and the alternate Olympics at Goodwood. Afterwards, I was to ride her other four horses, followed by teaching up to five private stu-dents as well as public students who trailered in for lessons. It was grueling work, but at the end of each week I was paid a percentage of the fees for the lessons I taught. However, I wasn't there to make money. My experience at Idlewilde was to serve as a useful opportunity to begin establishing contacts, as well as learning what it might take to return to America. Scouring ads in the local newspaper and asking around, I developed a feel for what the cost of renting an apartment and obtaining a car would be...everything necessary for me to begin my own business.

In the meantime, word had gotten out about my ability as a trainer, though thankfully not about my eloquence, as my command of the English language left quite a bit to be desired. I was now 28, and while my German was so fluent that I had sometimes been asked which part of Germany I was from, my English consisted of what I had learned in school, which I had barely used since my teen years. So trying to translate was not easy, to say the least. There is, for example, a slang phrase that Danish trainers commonly used when they were encouraging students to ride more forward: *"Rid ud af byen!"* This meant to ride forward as if being chased by the police out of town, but my fragmented and too-literal translation simply came out as me shouting, "Ride out of town! RIDE OUT OF TOWN!" Unsurprisingly, I was met by more than a few bewildered expressions. I may as well have been yelling, "THE BACON IS BURNT!" for the amount of sense it made to anyone. I learned quickly that the best way was to show students what I wanted instead of trying to tell them. Mounting the horses and riding them forward, up, and into the hand was a revelation for many, as they watched their horses transform before their eyes; and, most importantly, each student could feel the difference in the horse when they then got on themselves. Soon word was getting around, and I was meeting and teaching the public students that Linda allowed into her barn later in the day.

Two of the students I met would alter my life significantly—the first being Peggy Conroy. She was affable, fun to be with, and about the same age I was. Peggy was the sort of person I liked immediately, and although she had been riding with Ljungquist at the time, she took a few lessons from me and we had an instant, great connection. I had a good gut feeling when she told me her family was building a riding facility and arena in Plattsburg—60 miles south of Montreal— to see whether dressage training might be a profitable venture. At the time, I had no idea where Plattsburg was, but I was intrigued.

An organic plan fell into place. Linda had a horse for sale that Peggy thought she could sell. I don't know how she managed it, but somehow Peggy was able to convince Linda to give me the time off to accompany her, as she drove this horse to her farm in the biggest blue horse van I'd ever seen. I was getting used to the fact that everything was bigger in America—homes, cars, cities—but this horse van had its own gravitational pull. Smaller vehicles orbited around it. I had never ridden in anything so enormous, and spent the next ten hours chatting with Peggy and gazing out the window at the countryside flashing by.

We finally arrived at the family compound: one hundred acres, with a huge family scattered about in different houses. It was like the Waltons on steroids—a rustic idyll, with a barn built by the Conroy brothers that was certainly not lavish, but contained a functional 20 by 40-meter indoor with connecting stalls running down each side. The family worked hard and partied harder. Some of them shod their own horses, and a few of them flew their own planes. I'd never seen or met anyone like them. In the four days I was there, they had already arranged for me to teach lessons for two full days. Being able to "show and not tell" the students by riding their own horses to demonstrate what I wanted them to do, I was immediately well-received—and well-paid for my services.

Thanking Peggy's brother John, and his wife Liz, who, with Peggy, were the brains behind building the new stables, I was excited as I walked toward that behemoth of a blue van to begin the trek home to Linda's.

"You want to drive?" Peggy offered suddenly.

I hesitated a moment, looking up at the thing. "Sure," I replied.

Maybe I was still feeling the intoxicating effects of the "can do" approach of the Conroy clan, as I climbed up into the cab. Maybe I was feeling a bit of American brashness invading my brain. But clearly what I wasn't feeling was common sense, as I drove over the speed limit with only a Danish driver's license, and was promptly pulled over. My heart was pounding out of my chest with fear—how strict were American traffic laws? Peggy, however, as cool as a cucumber, calmly managed to both apologize—"I'm so sorry, but he doesn't speak

English"—and talk her way out of a fine. We were released with a stern warning, and as soon as we pulled back onto the road, she gave me a cheeky wink. That was Peggy to a "T."

The second student who was significant to my fortunes was Pat Shipley. Pat had a lovely farm, she said, with an arena, a beautiful common green-space area—and a rider named Debbie Johnson. She was more than willing to offer me a week of training and teaching at her place. I accepted, and it took me but three days to let it be known that I would find a way to return to the States. Debbie, with whom I worked well, said, "If I can help you, I'll do whatever it takes to train with you." It felt incredible to have this sort of support and encouragement from people I'd just met.

Back in Maryland, it wasn't long before Birgit arrived. To our surprise, we experienced a dose of American "family values." Although everyone knew we were a couple, in Linda's parents' house, we were expected to stay in separate bedrooms, as we weren't married. Thankfully, we were soon given a room in the home of one of the students I taught—Kathy, who, along with her husband Chuck, had slightly more liberal ideas about the sleeping arrangements of young couples. The generosity continued with Peggy loaning us her car so we could drive back and forth to the farm.

Peggy also spoke of the possibility of extending my stay and teaching in Plattsburg after my contract with Linda expired. She didn't have to ask twice. Birgit and I exchanged our return tickets to Denmark so that we would fly out of Montreal instead of D.C.

Regardless of the language barrier, my stay was a success. My dressage education and ability to train was admired, and not only was I treated with respect, I was also welcomed with open arms. The cultural difference was marked. I had come of age in the rigid, frosty formality of Germany and had already had to readjust to the more liberal tone of the Danes. And, oddly, while a liberal tone is apparent in Danish culture, so is a hesitancy to open up. This characteristic is best explained by Aksel Sandemose's book *A Fugitive Crosses His Tracks*, in which a common code of conduct within the fictional town of Jante is strictly adhered to, meant to explain the prevailing attitudes of Nordic countries. Without borrowing all ten rules in this code of conduct directly from Wikipedia, suffice it to say that this deeply-rooted set of standards, steeped in egalitarianism, includes never thinking you are anything special, or that you're more important than anyone else, and, most jarringly, you are not to think you are actually good—better than anyone else—at anything.

In my view, this perspective shuts down any opportunity, or even encouragement, for anyone to spread their wings, take a chance, or seek to improve their lot in life—in short, it precludes pursuing the "American Dream." For me, this very real attitude was yet another heavy contributor to how boxed-in I had been feeling in Denmark. Combined with what I had experienced in piles of required paper-work—even an issued "driver's record book," in which I was obliged to write down every mile I drove and to which destination—I was simply unwilling to believe this was the best that life had to offer. By contrast, in America, it is actually assumed you will try to improve yourself, and they love nothing more than a "rags to riches" story. Americans will applaud you, become inspired by you—they'll even name a street after you.

And in Denmark, you might make a new acquaintance, or get to know a colleague from work, but it likely will take quite some time before either person will begin to share more personal aspects of their lives. Not so in America. Not only was I greeted with open faces and enthusiasm, I found myself suddenly surrounded by people who, in no time at all, were comfortable telling me everything about themselves: their relationships, their families, their recent gallbladder surgery. It's one of the most appealing things about Americans, and it's something that makes life, and business, much easier. You know how people feel and where they stand. I found this—and still find this—incredibly refreshing.

The generosity and kindness was like nothing I had ever experienced. The parents of a student at Linda's—Theo and Lynn Peterson—invited me to their country club for dinner. Ordering a shrimp cocktail and a gin and tonic seemed extravagant; in Denmark, it was common to meet up with friends for dinner with everyone expected to pay their own way. But here, I was told to have what I liked, as a guest. Another couple invited me to go bar-hopping on their boat in Annapolis, while yet another had me to their house for Maryland crabs. I was blown away by the hospitality.

In the meantime, it almost felt as if I'd been adopted by the Conroy family. There was party after party after party. Even I threw a party at one of their homes! And if they weren't throwing parties, they were flying to parties. I would join them soaring over Lake Champlain, and will never forget the terror of being nonchalantly informed, "Uh, we gotta turn back because we're almost out of fuel." I had always assumed pilots checked that sort of thing before takeoff. (I guess this time it had been overlooked…) But for a young man like me, who had grown up in the era of post-war austerity in Europe, this was an entirely different way of life.

And I fell in love with it.

One of the last things Birgit and I did before returning to Denmark was attend a big horse show in Lake Placid. There was an abundance of Grand Prix jumpers. On our way, we drove by Jessica Ransehousen's farm, where, to our amazement, there was a heated indoor riding arena. We shook our heads in wonder, thinking of all those freezing winter mornings in Denmark. Gunnar Andersen had worked as a trainer at Jessica's for two years back in the 1960s. And now I was to follow in my mentor's footsteps. Nothing was going to stop me from applying for a visa at the American embassy in Denmark as soon as I returned.

CHAPTER
15

A PIONEER

N O SOONER HAD I RETURNED HOME than I was moving forward with plans to emigrate. It's a difficult, almost excruciating, thing not to be able to tell everyone such exciting news, but obtaining a visa was a lengthy process, and I couldn't risk hurting my established business at Frederiksdal. I did, however, inform a very close circle of friends—including my parents, who were less than enthusiastic about such a monumental move. In particular, my mother, with whom I had been very close all my life, was devastated.

"But America is so far away," she said. "Surely there are closer places to work?"

"I don't have the same opportunities for such success here," I tried to explain. "Everything is so much easier in America."

"Why have other Danish *bereiters* not done the same thing, if it is such a good idea?" she countered.

I didn't reply. I doubt she would have listened anyway. Had I moved from Southern Jutland to Northern Jutland, the distance would have been too far, in her opinion. She was losing her only child, and that was difficult for her—although once I was in America, both she and my father were only too happy to come for lengthy stays when I sent them airline tickets each year.

The other person with whom I was very close was, of course, Birgit. She had known of my desire to emigrate from the beginning; however, things were going very well for her at that time. She was becoming increasingly successful as a show jumper in Denmark and the Nordic countries, with her full-time job as a lab technician giving her the needed security to pursue her competitive career. And with my desire to emigrate to an uncertain future, it was clear that our lives were taking us in different directions. We did, of course, remain friends, and I was glad to hear that after I left, she sold Dorus to Germany's Herbert Krug, a rider for the German team and a well-known horse dealer in Frankfurt.

Her star was definitely on the rise.

In no time, I arrived at the most impressive building and address on Dag Hammarskjölds Alle in Copenhagen—the site of the American embassy. I wasn't quite sure what to expect, but after waiting quite some time in line, I was greeted warmly by a woman named Mrs. Elling. You might find it funny that I remember the name of a civil servant from so many decades ago; however, I tend to remember the people in my life who have been supportive, encouraging, or, in her case, made it possible for my emigration to be a success upon the first attempt.

Mrs. Elling asked whether I planned for my emigration to be permanent. Without hesitation, I replied yes. She then stressed that I must follow every rule to the letter in order to get my permanent green card and begin the process while I was in Denmark. Mrs. Elling pointed out how many people made the grave error of waiting until they were actually in the United States before applying for a visa, which made the whole process nearly impossible. I was beyond grateful, thanked her for her advice, and decided quickly to follow her recommendations.

There was a lot of work to be done. The Conroy family was kind enough to be my sponsors, doing most of the paperwork between Denmark and the United States. It took a solid nine months to put it all together, beginning that July of 1975, and the wait was interminable. It was, however, one of the most exciting periods of my life. And while the Conroy family was working hard on my behalf, I also had much to do on my side of the world.

One of the first things to take care of was signing a letter saying that I was not a Communist and that there had been no Communists in my family for many generations. I felt a slight panic, remembering my first girlfriend at the age of 15 whose father had been a member of the party. Surely that didn't count? I scarcely remembered the man.

Soon it was time for the physical examination, which would include X-rays of my chest to make sure I didn't have tuberculosis. Following Mrs. Elling's advice, I made an appointment with a doctor she recommended in Copenhagen, an older gentleman. I disliked him almost immediately: not only was he unctuous and negative, but I felt as though he was blatantly undermining my attempt to emigrate. Matter-of-factly, he assured me that if he found even the "slightest problem," I could wave goodbye to my American adventure. He proceeded to go over me with a fine-toothed comb, and when he came upon a very slight swelling, he declared it to be cancer and gave me a sanctimonious lecture about how I should stay in Denmark. I couldn't get out of there fast enough, and lined up another doctor for a second opinion. Thankfully, I was told I definitely did not have cancer and received the doctor's certification that I was in good health.

In those days of fax machines, before the internet, the wait was unbearable. I felt as if my life was on hold, even though each day was filled with training and teaching. Every evening, with hope in my heart, I opened the mailbox, and finally, in February of 1976, the letter from Liz and Peggy Conroy arrived. I ripped open the envelope and my eyes swept across the first line of their letter:

"All the paperwork taken care of and accepted; we look forward to seeing you."

I stood next to the mailbox, holding the letter in both hands, and let the long-awaited news wash over me, just as I had stood in front of my school all those years ago upon completing my final year. And the same thought returned: Now a whole new life has opened up ahead of me.

I was trying not to think about the short conversation I had had with Gunnar Andersen prior to receiving my green card. "I'm telling you this because I trust you and want to invite you over to America," I said to him one Wednesday.

Imagine my disappointment when he advised against it. "It's a huge country," he said.

This half-halt admittedly made me think, but not for long. Nothing, really, could stop me at this point—and in the end, both he and my lifelong friend Ina Zetterstrom, who has been indispensable for maintaining my relationships with my Frederiksdal friends at countless gatherings, saw me off at the airport.

However, there were important details to iron out beforehand. And the first of these was to inform Torben face-to-face that I was leaving his employment of seven years to move to America. I telephoned and asked to meet up with him. Whether he sensed something was amiss or not, I don't know, but he balked and pushed back, wanting to know what was so important that I couldn't just tell him over the phone. Cornered, I asked him what he would say if I quit Frederiksdal. Clearly thrown, Torben could only think of what might be considered his competition, which was a very small riding school in a rural area miles away; I can still remember his imperious tone as he said flatly, "If it is to work at Holstebro, then I cannot recommend it." I had to suppress a laugh. To his credit, when I explained to him about the possibilities for my future in the United States, he fully understood. After all, he was a driven businessman himself, and he could appreciate a sound business plan.

Finally, I could tell everyone around me the news. It was an enormous relief to release what had been excitedly bottled up within me for months. To put it mildly, there was an explosion of emotion when the news broke. In true Danish tradition, as the one leaving, I threw a farewell party with the help of Inge Merete, who had been a good friend for many years. Her breezy planning ensured the hall was filled with catered food and drink, and toward the end of the celebration, I gave a heartfelt speech of appreciation. I was touched by everyone's reactions, and they had also collected money for a Passier saddle, which I brought with me to the United States.

The next obligation before me was to return to my parents home in Haderslev, where I would collect some things I had stored in their basement as well as my old friend, the wicker trunk. Filled with all my belongings, including my new saddle, it was sent ahead to America by ship.

The final few days before my departure were a blur, there were so many things to be done. Besides saying goodbye to family and friends,

I had to pack, and pick up all the paperwork, including the X-rays of my lungs. Today, these would look comical—the X-rays were enormous, the size of poster boards, and had to be carried by hand, with extreme care not to crush or fold them in any way. My final task was delivering my car, which I had sold, to its new owners on my last day in Denmark.

I don't think I actually exhaled until I found my seat after boarding the plane to America. That memory is as sharp as if it occurred yesterday—everything felt nearly too good to be true. After nearly a year of waiting for the paperwork, tests, and signatures (not to mention being deeply affected after seeing a paper signed by dozens of riders I'd taught in the States, petitioning for my return and promising work), I was actually on my way to a whole new life, and nothing could stop me now. My excitement was overwhelming, and I was even proud of myself for having the courage to undertake such a big decision to change my life.

In a way, I felt somewhat like a pioneer. To the best of my knowledge, I was the first educated *berider*—I chose now the Danish spelling of the better-known German term—with the exams and papers to prove it to choose to move permanently to the United States. Waiting impatiently for everyone to board and for the plane to begin to taxi toward the runway, I suddenly heard my name called out over the loudspeaker, and my heart began to pound. Dear God, was something wrong with my papers? Had I left something out? Neither—my name had been called because two of my students, Irene and Anja, in a lovely gesture, had ordered champagne as a surprise for me on the plane. It didn't get any better than that. Later, after the plane reached its cruising altitude and the flight attendants came down the aisle with the drinks trolley, I smiled as my crystal glass (not plastic in those days!) was filled with the sparkling pale gold liquid.

Glancing at the vastness of the Atlantic outside my window, I toasted the view. Nothing could be more exciting in my life than this moment.

CHAPTER
16

ON THE ROAD

DISEMBARKED IN MONTREAL, carrying my entire world in my suitcase: clothes, riding boots, and $4,000. I wandered through the terminal a bit nervously, looking for my ride. I glanced at my watch—had I mistakenly given the Conroys the wrong date or time of arrival? Killing time, I checked for the hundredth time that I had everything in order for my next destination, the Office of Immigration, where my cherished green card awaited me at the Canadian/United States border.

At last I saw John, gave a happy wave, and, gathering up my things, we headed out to his car. Upon arriving at the border, I wanted to blow a kiss across the ocean to Mrs. Elling, who had stressed the importance of having all my paperwork in order before I left Denmark, for I sailed through Immigration without a hitch. I was somewhat surprised, even disappointed, that my prized X-rays, too large to be packed and having remained in my hands the entire trip, were never given even a cursory glance. Evidently there was no concern about tuberculosis. Or ebola, for that matter. Call me sentimental, but I didn't throw those X-rays away until around 2015. I suppose they represented part of the exciting new life to which I had looked forward for so long.

In true Conroy fashion, I was greeted by the family with open arms, and I had barely unpacked when they invited everyone in the area who had an interest in dressage for a large gathering at their lodge. This "Meet Gunnar" party drew people from as far away as Montreal, and could not have been a better start for my own business. In fact, one gentleman who attended, George Pelletier, enquired upon shaking my hand whether I would come to Montreal each Wednesday to teach 10 riders. He didn't have to ask twice. In the meantime, the Conroys' generosity extended to finding me an apartment to rent, and assisting me with getting my social security card, a phone (which involved my first experience with a "party line," as I attempted not only to schedule lessons, but, with my limited English, to understand Anne Gribbons's Swedish, as she wanted to come up to board and take a few lessons while attending the Montreal Games), and, most importantly, my largest investment yet: a new car. Well, new to me.

I had parted with my faithful red Volkswagen upon departing Denmark, and it was John, who knew of a dealership in the area, who helped me with the purchase of my first American car. As everything else in America was big—the country, the buildings, the highways—it seemed only reasonable that my car be comparable in size. And it was. For $1,750, I purchased a 1973 Dodge with a hood that was so long it was in another timezone. After my four-cylinder Beetle, the roar of the eight cylinders I now owned felt akin to blasting off from Cape Canaveral each time I stepped on the accelerator—that is, once I learned to drive it.

It's probably amusing to most Americans, but Europeans grow up driving stick-shift, and in those days, it was all that was available. So to sit on the vast bench seat of my Dodge, with its padded steering wheel, endless dash display of knobs, and no stick shift was somewhat intimidating. Luckily, I had John next to me to give me my first and only lesson.

"Okay," he said. "Take your left foot and put it way over to the left."

I did as directed.

"Now leave it there," he added. "You'll never use it again."

That, and a quick explanation of how to shift the gear lever into drive, neutral, or park, was all that was needed. I was on my own, and soon on my way for the two-and-a-half-hour drive to teach my first clinic in Montreal. It didn't matter that my car got roughly two city blocks to the gallon when a gallon only cost 45 cents. The mere thought of driving on the busy North American highways with their perplexing lanes and exits made me a nervous wreck the night before I departed, and I was so stressed by it all that I decided, "Okay, I'm just going to drive as slowly as I need to so I don't miss my exit."

In those days before GPS, all I had was a gas station map I was trying to unfold and glance at as I drove, and street signs I could barely read. I drove as slowly as a hearse on the highway—probably 30 mph—and didn't realize I was being tailgated by a long line of cars who had no intention of going to a funeral. Finally, one car made a bold move to roar past me, but not before pulling up alongside and yelling a lungful of profanities at me. Yes, I wore glasses, but no, I was certainly not "f***ing Mr. Magoo."

It's been said that you know you've made the right choice when doors that were previously closed to certain dreams are seemingly flung wide open, and so it seemed to me, as I was inundated with work from the get-go. Shortly after the clinic in Montreal, I flew to Maryland to teach again. Boarding that plane, I had a flashback to hearing about a trainer who flew to his various clients, when I was an apprentice in Flensburg.

How impressed I had been—and now here I was, flying: from Plattsburgh to Saranac Lake, then on to Albany. From Albany to D.C, for a clinic set up by Pat Shipley. I had hit the ground running, and was teaching 10 students a day, with many people I had previously taught at Linda Zang's.

As soon as I finished teaching at Pat's, I was picked up the following day by Ellen Holm—who, now that she had divorced and returned to the States, went by her maiden name, Shepherd—and her then-boyfriend, and soon-to-be husband, Bill McKee, to teach at her place.

Ellen was really the only friend I had in the States at that time, and I was more than touched that she had arranged a birthday party for me.

These days seemed to pass in a blur. Sandy Howard came for a lesson. She had traveled from California to work with Colonel Ljung quist, and happened to be in the area. At that time, trainers who could teach riders at the FEI level were few and far between. Many riders, therefore, traveled great distances to get the best instruction. Sandy had an amazing horse that had an impressive piaffe and passage. However, flying changes were not working well, so she had come to me. My English was still a long way from fluent, but we soon understood each other and had a strong working relationship that continued for many years. She was a regular participant when I later taught in California.

A day later, I flew back to Plattsburgh, and, looking forward to a good night's sleep, I was dismayed to find my flight was delayed; I decided to call John to ask if he might pick me up from the airport. I had not, however, tried my hand at using an American payphone. Frustrated with fumbling and failing, I was about to give up in despair when an elderly gentleman, sensing my desperation, approached to ask if I needed help. Gratefully, I tried to explain that I had emigrated from Denmark and needed to call a friend. He nodded, showed me how to proceed with answering the operator's questions, and handed the phone back to me. I'll never forget him then reaching up to pat my shoulder gently, saying, "Young man, you are welcome here." His kind assistance and the warmth of his words left such a strong impression upon me that I found myself writing to my parents a couple of days later to share the experience. Over the years, I have received an abundance of hospitality from complete strangers in this country, and it remains one of the things about America I love best.

John soon arrived and immediately asked how the clinic had gone and how much I'd earned. This had nothing to do with being nosey; he was truly excited for my success, and when he learned that I was earning a thousand dollars a week (a huge amount in those days!), he would roar with laughter. He had such a contagious laugh, I found myself laughing alongside him. He was genuinely happy for me, and this was so unlike what I had experienced in Denmark—the expectation that you would never reveal your success, and would even be somewhat embarrassed by it—that it was a revelation to allow myself to be excited by how well everything was going.

I couldn't wait to get to my apartment and collapse into bed. But John had different ideas: unbeknownst to me, I was to celebrate turning 30 twice and was being driven straight to a surprise birthday party that had been arranged in my absence. How could I say no? Yes, I was utterly exhausted, but I was also blown away by the goodness being shown to me—particularly being introduced to an important member of the poultry (and whiskey) family: a Mr."Wild Turkey." Perhaps the less said about that, the better, but it was certainly a memorable night.

At this point I must beg the pardon of the reader if what follows sounds as though I am dropping names. I can assure you that is not my intention—what I desire to convey is a sense of how these nonstop, work-laden weeks seemed to lead me on a path that crossed with some of the biggest names in the equestrian world, beginning with two women who were arguably the most influential in American dressage: Jessica Ransehousen, and "Sis" Steinkraus, the wife of Olympic gold medalist Bill Steinkraus.

My mentor Gunnar Andersen indirectly helped me get Jessica as a client. She had been taught by Gunnar when she was in Copenhagen. Later, he had worked for her for two years at her own facility. Now, she had written to him asking whether he would recommend working with me. I found out much later from Gunnar's wife Gerda that he had replied to her to say that not only had I recently won the prestigious Danish Professional Rider's Championship, but I was the best young berider in Denmark.

All of this was unknown to me when Jessica telephoned and asked if she could come over and watch me ride. For whatever reason, she canceled twice before finally keeping the third appointment. Keen to appear professional and unruffled, I made certain I was riding one of the top horses the Conroys had—a Swedish Warmblood owned by Liz, who was barely schooling at 3rd Level but was a big mover. I was hoping she would get the best possible impression of me. She did, and I will always remember how sweet she was from that very first meeting. I can't describe the feeling when she invited me to her farm to ride and teach her.

To be honest, Jessica had much more experience than I did in those days. She was a talented rider with a résumé that boasted a lot of impressive accomplishments. She had been trained by both Gunnar Andersen and Reiner Klimke in Germany, had competed throughout Europe, and had ridden in the Olympics. I think it was mostly me who learned something from her. But she was gracious enough to handle the subject tactfully, and let me ride her horses and teach her. When I helped her warm up for competitions, I could feel the eyes of the other trainers and competitors upon me. Being in Jessica's orbit brought extra attention in the best possible way. If I was skilled enough to help Jessica Ransehousen, then there were also others in the American dressage community that I could help. And one of them was Sis Steinkraus.

In between interruptions on the party line of my phone from two women discussing a recent hysterectomy, I received a call from Sis, whom I always addressed as "Mrs. Steinkraus," and with whom I immediately felt a good feeling. She was warm and good-natured, and asked if I would come to teach a clinic at her and Bill's estate at Great Island in Darien, Connecticut. I didn't need to pull out my diary before readily agreeing. My impulsive reply turned to horror when she then casually said, "Good—you just fly into La Guardia, get a limo, and we'll pick you up at the Howard Johnson's." My heart pounded at the thought of being overwhelmed by that airport, and a "limo" meant being crammed inside with as many as a dozen other passengers and suffering through a dozen stops before reaching my destination.

I summoned the courage to put my foot down and insist, "No, no, you've got to pick me up from the airport!" I could feel her smile over the line as she agreed everything would be taken care of, and it was—when I arrived, there was a driver holding a large card with my name on it. I was swept into the back of the town car and taken to the Steinkraus estate.

Sis's family had made a fortune from, if I remember correctly, something as simple as baking soda, yet their home wasn't a mansion. As the driver negotiated the bridge to get to the island and the barn, my impression was that the Steinkraus estate wasn't unlike the historic equestrian landmark of Gladstone. Large, and it was indeed elegant, appointed beautifully with antiques, but also warm and even cozy. There was nothing ostentatious about it. The stables, however, held me in awe: they wouldn't have been out of place in Europe, constructed of stone, including a coach house. A covered arena had been added in an attractive, fluid extension, and there was an outdoor arena that was placed very close to Long Island Sound. Taking it all in, it occurred to me that once again I was following in the footsteps of

Gunnar Andersen, as he had taught clinics here as well. It goes without saying that everything was immaculate.

Upon speaking to Peggy Conroy about the writing of this book, she mentioned that I used to refer to myself as "a little Danish guy with a big American dream." I actually have no memory of saying that, but I will say that being seated for dinner between this cultured and congenial couple as a guest in their home, this "little Danish guy" knew he was in the middle of one of life's golden moments.

The clinic was full, with ten riders a day, and I remember Gary Rockwell being one of them. This success also helped my growing reputation, and when I look back at my day book from the time—which I still have—I am astonished by my teaching schedule. Yes, I was young, fit, and hungry for success, but the truth of it was that I was doing the work of two, or even three, people. I was constantly on the road, teaching weekly in Montreal, and then off to Maryland, followed by Syracuse—which came about because of a couple who were to become good friends of mine: Pat and Jerry Stone.

I had met the Stones on my first trip to the States, and had learned that Jerry had been to Germany as a young man, where he had ridden and trained. Having these roots in common, we got along very well together, and now that I was in America full time, they offered to introduce me to friends of theirs, the Stantons, who had a stable in Syracuse, New York, where I might be able to teach. I remember having just gotten home from Montreal and not even having a chance to do laundry before I loaded up with them in their Volkswagen and headed out on this next trip to meet potential new business partners.

What awaited me was a large stable with an equally large arena. It was my first encounter with what would turn out to be a common occurrence in the States: the wife being the rider or trainer, while the husband was the groundskeeper and farrier. Often the stables were cleaner than the house itself, and that fact remains an inside joke with many riders today. The Stantons and I agreed that I would teach there, and their daughter, Lori, even worked for me a few years later. But, oh, how quickly I learned that I had bitten off almost more than I could chew. I had excitedly agreed to teach one of my first clinics there. With my broken English, teaching ten 45-minute lessons was hard enough, but desperately trying to get at least a couple of horses on the bit, all the while being distracted by a dozen loose chickens running through the arena, was something else.

There was a big horse show being held in Syracuse while we were there, so we decided to attend. Pat pointed out George Morris to me in hushed tones, and I remembered his name from Gunnar Andersen, who had taught him a few times at Jessica's. Since that time, I had read in several horse magazines that the meeting between the two had meant something pretty special to George Morris.

Impulsively I decided that I would greet him, despite Pat and Jerry strenuously advising me not to. After all, George Morris was the best-known rider at the time. As an Olympic medalist, he was equestrian royalty, and people like me couldn't just blithely stride up and say hello. Except I did.

With my pipe in my mouth (I only found out much later that George detested anything to do with smoking), I approached him. Putting out my hand, I said, "Hello, my name is Gunnar Ostergaard. Do you remember Gunnar Andersen?"

There was a pause before he looked me up and down and replied in his slow voice, "Do I remember him? He is without a doubt one of the greatest horsemen I have ever met in my life."

What followed was a long, pleasant conversation, and we even exchanged numbers before parting. Pat and Jerry stood some distance away, agog at what had just transpired. They were so thrilled for me that they took me out to dinner on the way home to hear all about it.

My days consisted of rising while it was still dark and driving off to teach as the sun rose. I had everything: countless clients, a steady income, and good friends. The only thing I didn't have, and longed for, was a nap. Around this same time, I had taken out a full page ad in the magazine *Dressage & Combined Training*, announcing my arrival and availability for training. Almost immediately, I received a call from a gentleman in California, who left a message on my answering machine enquiring about having me come west to teach a clinic. Eager to give every appearance of being professional, I promptly returned his phone call first thing the following morning—completely forgetting the three-hour time difference. Groggy, as anyone would be at four o'clock in the morning, he replied, "Maybe you can call back a little later." I cringed when I looked at my own clock, realizing what I'd done. In the end, it worked out, but on the condition that I commit to two weeks, as it wasn't financially worth his while for anything less. I was at the point in my career where I didn't dare turn anything down—even though I'd barely begun at Plattsburgh, I hastily agreed.

The clinic was held at Stanford University in northern California, as part of their riding program. For two weeks, I was teaching 10 lessons a day and completely drained by evening. My English was still limited, and what little I knew was coming out hoarse; as per usual, the most effective way for me to get across what I wanted to teach was by riding the horses.

One memorable lesson was with Mimi Dickerson, who had brought a horse that she had described as "difficult to manage," as he was quite spooky. In my view, the horse simply wasn't on the bit—and so I rode this horse round and round, and there was never a single spook. She couldn't believe it. At one point, I instructed Mimi to actually try and make him spook.

Hysterically, she hid behind a tree and then jumped out, yelling, "BOO!" just as I rode past, and the horse didn't flinch. Didn't even cock an ear.

Mission accomplished!

Because I was being driven around and teaching at different places, I was put up in various peoples' houses—not ideal, as I've always cherished my privacy. I was treated like royalty, being taken out to lovely restaurants, receiving heady feedback, but oh, how I longed for a single hour to myself! I was losing my voice, but I was obliged to continue to "chat" when I was taken out for meals. One student's husband was an erudite professor at Stanford, and an expert on Danish history. As we were seated for dinner, I can only assume he thought I was agreeing with him, as I nodded blankly while he gave me a full account of the origins of my mother country, from the 8th century to Hamlet. I hadn't traced the royal lineage back to the Viking kings, Gorm the Old and Harald Bluetooth, and frankly I never would. I just wanted a beer and a bed. Imagine how I sighed with relief the following day, when I was told I had been checked into a rather upscale hotel.

This, I later learned, was only to keep my presence a secret from Hilda Gurney, who was a regular clinician in the area. I can't think it ever bothered her, as we've always been on good terms.

To be fair, there were some lovely homes in which I stayed. I remember one in Pebble Beach with a sweeping view of the golf course. I was so impressed by being given sausages for breakfast, I later phoned my mother to relay this novelty. She laughed—it simply wasn't done in my family, and seemed terribly indulgent at the time. If I thought breakfast sausage was special, imagine my reaction when my hosts, Mr. King Harris and his wife Elizabeth, announced they would like to fly two of their horses across the country to be in full training with me. During this time, in the late 1970s, such an undertaking was virtually unheard of.

Upon arriving home to Plattsburgh, trying to shake off the jet lag, I was schooling one of the horses I had in training when an official-looking car drove into the yard. Two men in nondescript suits got out and abruptly asked to see my green card. I dismounted and put the horse away; even though I had all the necessary paperwork in order, my heart was beating out of my chest. They followed me to my apartment, where I fumbled around for the key to the door. I couldn't find it, and, trying to stifle the panic rising in my throat, I must have appeared very suspicious. The key, of course, was in my other pocket, and in the end I managed to unlock the door, gather my papers, and show my green card to them. Everything was fine; I began to calm down, and I even found myself asking them if I could change my address. This was the first time I had articulated this thought, and these government men replied that that was no problem as long as I paid my taxes. They departed, leaving me deep in my own thoughts.

I had great affection and appreciation for the Conroys. They had been the catalyst for making it possible for me to come to America. And yet in order to make a living, I knew I couldn't stay. Yes, I was earning what was considered at the time to be an eye-popping sum, $1,000 per week, but only because I was constantly traveling. When I specify that this $1,000 was earned by my charging the going rate of $20 per lesson, that perhaps gives a clearer picture of the density of my schedule. It made no sense to be based at a place that provided maybe 5 percent of my income. Despite our best efforts, the truth of the matter was that there simply wasn't a large enough demographic of dressage riders in the Plattsburgh area, leaving me to essentially live on the road. I don't exaggerate when I say it made more sense to put up a cot in the airport than to remain in Plattsburgh. I had only been there for five months, yet each day I woke up exhausted.

Something had to give.

CHAPTER
17

HOLST-KNUDSEN

THE WEEKS WENT BY IN A BLUR. I was still teaching in Maryland, Syracuse, and Montreal, and sometime in April, I received an invitation to teach in Charlotte, Vermont, directly across Lake Champlain from Plattsburgh. Liz Conroy encouraged me to accept, telling me it was a beautiful area and even the ferry ride across the lake would be enjoyable. She was right—Vermont was "love at first sight" for me, and I knew instantly that this was a state I wanted to explore. It was the most beautiful landscape I'd ever seen, and I was enchanted. The undulating deep green hills and mountain ranges were refreshing after the comparatively flat terrain of Plattsburgh, and everywhere I looked was a feast for the eyes. Happily, there were, and have been, several repeat opportunities to teach at lovely farms along the charming, unpaved roads that wound through its countryside.

Even today, I still know some of the riders I worked with there in the past, such as Madeleine Austin (mother of Liz), who rode in those early clinics, which were put together by Betty Ann Welsh. Ellen Miller had facilities in Burlington, Vermont, as did Mike Mause, and I still enjoy traveling to work with Ellen's students at Catie Wasserman's farm.

I had been squirreling away as much of my income as I could, and I was certainly not an extravagant spender. However, after teaching my third clinic in the area, I was ravenous, and before taking the ferry back toward New York, I decided to treat myself for once. The sun was just setting over the Adirondacks when I stopped in Essex, on the New York side of Lake Champlain, to ask a guy where I could find a really good restaurant for a nice meal. Glancing dubiously at me through the window of my Dodge, its sides covered with dust from the dirt roads, he pointed out a well-known restaurant, "The Old Dock," which sat at the water's edge on Lake Champlain, with a breathtaking view across the water. With a raised eyebrow, he mentioned tersely that it was "very expensive," the subtext being that there was no way someone like me could afford such an establishment. I thanked him, and with a wallet filled with clinic cash, I headed to the place and indulged in the obligatory shrimp cocktail of that era, followed by a medium-rare filet mignon and a superb glass of wine. I parted with an eye-watering $19 to pay for it all—nearly the price of a lesson! I'll never forget that bill, as it was the first time I'd rewarded myself with an evening of fine dining, and I felt as though I'd earned every bite. I'm also happy to say that "The Dock" is still there today, and just as good as it ever was.

Perhaps this experience was an omen that more good things were to come from Vermont, as it was also there that I purchased my first horse in America. Grand Cru was both named after and colored like champagne. I made a deal with the owner that I would pay half the purchase price of $1,500 in cash, and teach for the rest. Grand Cru quickly proved to be easy to ride, and when the summer was over, I sold him for a solid profit.

Debbie Johnson had remained my student and friend, and eventually became my barn manager. Because I still wasn't great at finding my way around, I was grateful that she accompanied me to Gladstone to watch the final selection trial for the Montreal Olympics. There were riders and friends I had hoped to see, among them Sandy Howard.

Sandy still had the horse with the impressive piaffe and passage, but issues remained with his flying changes, and unfortunately they were present on that particular day as well. Despite not being named to the team for Montreal, she was kind enough to introduce me—or should I say, to try to introduce me—to 1972 Olympian John Winnett, who would go on to be named as a reserve rider that year for Montreal. He had a terrific horse named Leopardi. John had brought the horse with him from Germany, where he had been trained by my good friend Herbert Rehbein. As Sandy marched up with me in tow, he was actually on the horse and not looking particularly approachable.

"John, do you have a moment? I'd like you to meet—"

Before she could even finish her introduction, he said curtly, "No, not really," before turning smartly to ride away!

It should be said that John and I actually became good friends afterward, and he later explained to me that during that time, he was being introduced to anyone who had even been near Europe, so he tended to nip all attempts in the bud.

A chance encounter later on at the hotel with one of the judges, a man by the name of Col. Summer whom I had known quite well in Denmark, led to him graciously including me in a blurb within his widely read monthly column in Denmark's biggest horse magazine: "Gunnar Ostergaard is doing well in America, and teaching a lot of clinics." A short line, for sure, but it felt like a pretty big validation of the path I'd chosen.

Returning to my tight schedule, I was now working overtime in order to carve out a few days off to host my first guest from Denmark, Per. I was eager to see him, as we'd known each other for years, ever since I had arrived at Frederiksdal. He was not a horse guy in the least—I'd gotten to know him through his sister, who rode with me.

Per was studying biology at university, and truly was a "jack of all trades." He was smart, good at sports, and an excellent photographer. In fact, he took the photograph of me riding that I used for both advertisements I'd taken out in *Dressage & Combined Training.* He had the ability to be immediately at ease with people, and could start a conversation with anyone. Per became interested in dressage simply because there were so many girls, and they, in turn, looked assessingly at his long, flowing hair, tie-dyed T-shirts, and frayed jeans. It was the '70s, and Per had embraced the hippie look, from the length of the hair on his head all the way to his toes, shod in Birkenstock sandals.

Per accompanied me up to Montreal to teach, and then to a dinner for the Montreal Dressage Association, where I was to give a speech. What possessed me to think I could give a speech with my halting delivery of English, I do not know, as I was still best at speaking if a horse was actually in front of me. However, in this instance, I was to comment on different horses and riders in a film being projected onto a screen before the audience. I began to stutter nervously, until

I heard Per call out from the back of the room in a loud voice, "What rider is that?" The image on the projector at that moment was of me riding, of course, and as everyone burst into laughter, I became far more relaxed.

As Per wanted to see more of the USA, we armed ourselves with maps and drove from Plattsburgh to Maryland, even playing tourist in Washington, D.C. Enjoying his stay immensely, Per wanted to stay longer to experience the Olympics in Montreal. For such a smart guy, he'd been a little lackadaisical in regards to his visa—he wasn't sure when it would expire. And this would prove to be our undoing.

At what should have been a routine stop at the border, when Canadian officials saw that his visa had indeed expired, we were ordered at once to pull into this hangar-type garage with metal tables, and were told, "Get out of the car!" Their tone was brusque, and we were immediately fearful. We were required to empty our pockets, and while I still looked not unlike a junior accountant in their eyes, Per evidently had "drug mule" written all over him. For two hours, we were subjected to the officials barking accusing questions at us, which we nervously tried to answer. At one point, they asked Per for his mother's maiden name, which was "Holst-Knudsen"—when spoken in a thick, Danish accent, this proved impossible for the officials to repeat or spell. He must have repeated "Holst-Knudsen" half a dozen times, even dragging it out as slowly as possible: "Hoooolst-Knuuuud-sennnn," and I found myself biting the inside of my cheek, trying not to laugh, while at the same time shoving my hands into my pockets to still their shaking. We were being threatened with arrest and there was absolutely nothing funny about that.

They were so sure that we were hiding something that my car was taken apart. Everything was pulled out of the trunk, and they even removed the front and back seats and dumped them on the ground while they rifled through every nook and cranny, intent on finding a stash of drug paraphernalia.

Of course, we were completely innocent, but we were both shaking like leaves, especially after one of the cops finally snapped, "It's only because my boss is in a good mood that we're not sending you to jail in Buffalo. Now, get outta here." With that, they both turned and left us standing alone in this cavernous building, car seats still upside down on the ground along with everything we'd stored in the trunk. After figuring out how to reinstall the seats, we drove carefully away for several miles before gunning the engine to return to Plattsburgh, where we decided a party to celebrate our freedom at the Conroy lodge was in order. First on the guest list was my acquaintance "Mr. Wild Turkey," and after a bit of a sore head the following morning, Per decided to get the hell out of Dodge soon after, returning to Denmark.

CHAPTER
18

LONG VALLEY

DEBBIE JOHNSON WAS ONLY TOO AWARE that I had been burning the candle at both ends, as I returned to my full schedule of non-stop traveling for work. We came to a decision. I had to find an address in which I could actually sleep in my own bed on occasion, and Debbie would manage the barn, with the continued opportunity to teach lessons and train a few horses as well. As anyone with horses will tell you, you can't give notice at a stable without having another position lined up, so come September, she discreetly placed an ad in *The Chronicle of the Horse* that read, "Dressage trainer seeking training facility for rent in NJ, PA."

There were two responses. One included a grainy photo of a tiny indoor arena somewhere in Ohio, which was lit by a single suspended light bulb hanging from the rafters in the middle. Pass. The second response was, frankly, staggering. My eyes flew over the typewritten lines describing a newly built 32-horse facility with a huge indoor arena and lovely paddocks. Best of all, not only was a house included—which would be appropriate for Debbie—but its location, on top of Schooley's Mountain, was in Long Valley, New Jersey, which was a mere half-hour from Gladstone. I couldn't wait to see it.

The timing was perfect: there was a show in the area to which I took a group of riders to compete in a "club" class. Peggy and Liz Conroy, as well as Jerry Stone, rode together in the required 3rd-Level test, competing with several other teams of riders and earning the highest combined score; they were elated to win. It was a big class, and a big deal. On a high, Debbie and I left the show on Saturday and drove over to meet with the owners of the Long Valley facility: Charles and Barbara Trillich. Charles had built the place for his daughters, who were into eventing and now had their own separate barn. Being a businessman, Charles saw the opportunity in building another barn—the one I hoped to lease—to earn its keep in rent.

Besides the fact that they were the nicest people I could hope to work with, the stable more than lived up to their description. The rent would be $1,800 per month—a massive risk for me, but I believed in my own work ethic and they evidently believed in me. With a handshake to seal our agreement, it was arranged that I would be taking over the stable by mid-October.

There was very little time to celebrate, as directly after the meeting, Debbie and I had to drive to yet another clinic I had scheduled at Pat Shipley's. I'd done this each month for five months, followed by another return clinic in Montreal. Both of these clinics were always full, with a waiting list. There was certainly no shortage of work, and any nervousness about earning that monthly nut of $1,800 at Long Valley began to dissipate, especially with the wealth of local dressage enthusiasts in the area.

There was much to do, and during all of it I was still teaching all over, but the one thing I didn't look forward to doing was informing the Conroys that I was leaving. I broke the news first to John; he was understandably disappointed, but he also realized my dilemma—it made no sense to be based in an area where there was simply not enough work. What I didn't know was that John, in his turn, would inform Liz of my impending departure on the day of her birthday. She was less than happy about it, and let me know by later approaching me to say, "Hey, thanks for the birthday present, Gunnar." That felt like the flick of a riding crop, but of course I understood her feelings. It is all water under the bridge these days, and they were gracious enough to accept my consolatory offer to return monthly to teach clinics. It was both quite sad as well as a relief to leave Plattsburgh. And by mid-October, as planned, I began working out of Long Valley.

An invitation from Sis Steinkraus to teach another clinic was a much-needed ray of sunshine, especially when she added, "Meet me in the box"—of course they had a box!—"at the National Horse Show at Madison Square Garden, and we'll drive you home to Great Island with us."

As luck would have it, one of my clients from Long Valley had business in New York City and offered to drive me into town. Pulling over to drop me off in front of the Garden, he instructed me to take my suitcase and go downstairs, where I could stow it in a row of lockers in the basement. I found myself on my own at two in the afternoon, with hours to kill before it would be time to meet Sis and Bill at seven. Feeling out of my element, but excited, I walked for blocks and blocks, taking in the energetic buzz of the city with all its shops and cafes, while carefully avoiding 42nd Street as I'd been warned to do.

Arriving promptly back at the Garden at seven o'clock, I joined the Steinkrauses in their private box to watch the Grand Prix Jumping. It was a fantastic evening, despite one cringeworthy moment when Kathy Kusner dropped by our box to say hello to Sis and Bill. I was still learning the names of all the American equine celebrities, but evidently hadn't gotten up to the Ks, so when Sis introduced me to Kathy, my reply—"You ride, too?"—earned me a sharp dig in the ribs from Sis's elbow. Once I recovered from this faux pas, however, I had a wonderful time, and at the end of the night, Sis suggested, "Run down and get your suitcase and we'll wait for you at the main entrance." No problem—hurriedly, I retrieved my suitcase from the locker, rushing as I didn't want to make them wait. And then, inexplicably, I simply could not find my way back up! The only escalators that I could see were coming down, carrying the relentless stream of 20,000 people who had just attended the show. It was ridiculous, but there was no "up" escalator in sight, and I rushed back and forth once more in panicked search of one before impulsively jumping onto one of the "down" ones, running against this tide of people—all of whom, I'm quite sure, thought I had escaped from Bellevue. I was panting, sweating, elbowing my way up, and the whole time I couldn't stop thinking about how I was inconveniencing my generous hosts by making them wait.

Halfway up, I heard someone say, "This guy's got a long way to go..." He was right. In the end, I made Sis and Bill wait for 15 minutes—it felt like an hour—and they were polite enough not to ask why I was breathing as if I'd just finished second at Pimlico. Silently, I got into the back of the car, and they returned me to Darien.

The late 1970s were a whirlwind for me, beginning with 1976, which was very much a year of firsts: my first top facility, my first sponsor, my first nightmare, and my first time getting shafted on a business deal—ironically, by a fellow Dane!

Each morning, driving into Long Valley, knowing this beautiful barn and indoor arena was mine, was the best feeling in the world—especially being only minutes away from Gladstone, which meant a lot to me. As always, in time, the rose-colored glasses come off to reveal an unwelcome surprise or two...the main one being that when I had agreed to take over the Long Valley stable on that warm September afternoon, it hadn't occurred to me that, come winter, regular snow plowing would be required, and I would be obliged to pay. Hundreds. This was an expensive lesson learned. However, the good far outweighed the bad.

I had come to know Marty and Holly Simensen through teaching. Marty's reputation as a top veterinarian, national Team vet, and all-around great guy was well deserved. Holly was Canadian, and after auditing one of my Wednesday clinics in Montreal, she approached me while I was still based at the Conroys' and offered to give me a horse to ride and show: Glass Owl. He was a tall, lanky chestnut, an ex-racehorse, and he followed me to Long Valley. I still feel very sentimental about Glass Owl, especially as he was to become the first horse that I would compete in my first dressage show in the States, held in New Jersey. He did me proud: entered into two 3rd-Level classes, he won them both, bringing home a hatful of blue ribbons. I enjoyed training him, and he was coming along nicely.

In an utterly tragic twist of fate, months later Glass Owl would suffer a freak accident in the middle of the night, requiring him to be immediately euthanized. Having received word from the night security guard, I had rushed over, and was devastated. Now I hesitated, heart in my throat, to dial the phone and give Holly the dreadful news at two in the morning. No trainer ever wants to have to make that sort of call, and yet the first words that this incredibly kind and understanding woman spoke after digesting what I had relayed to her were, "Don't worry—I will get you another horse." How anyone could put someone else's feelings over their own at such a terrible time was, and still is, beyond me, but that was Holly, and I will always be grateful to her.

Things began to look up again as I started teaching clinics at George Morris's Hunterdon Farm, a half-hour away. No one in the hunter world, of course, was a bigger name than George, and for it to be known that I was teaching all his upper level riders (who, by the way, impressed me with their understanding of straightness and technique) meant that, come winter, I was teaching at all the top hunter barns in the area.

On the heels of all this work, there seemed to be yet another terrific opportunity lining up for me. While at Long Valley, I had learned that there was a Danish dressage judge living in the area. Gunnar Andersen had done a clinic or two at her place, and she decided to trailer over for a few lessons with her Swedish Warmblood, who was schooling 3rd Level. I felt the horse had plenty of talent but obviously needed much more training. We agreed that if she would pay his board, I would do all the training for free, in exchange for having the opportunity to compete him the following spring. I kept my side of the bargain by riding the horse daily, and was feeling pretty enthusiastic about how he was progressing.

Looking forward to going to the upcoming shows with something really rather impressive to compete, I was left open-mouthed when one day, out of the blue, she announced that she would be taking him back home.

"But we talked about this—me training him for free all this time so that I could show him in the spring!" I said, flabbergasted.

"Well," she agreed, "we talked about it..." and then she let the rest of the sentence die away.

She took the horse away, with heaps of correct training now in place. I couldn't believe anyone could be so brazenly dishonest. In the end, I suppose that in every life, a little rain—or should I say a little Dane—must fall.

CHAPTER
19

HALF THE ELECTRIC BILL

THE YEAR 1977 BEGAN WITH A BANG. While my first winter at Long Valley—perched atop a mountain—was a tough one, with the added snowplowing expenses, I had so much business that I found myself in the fortunate position of being able to pick and choose when and where I wanted to teach or train. I was in need of another working student to assist with the load, and placing an ad in *The Chronicle* led to several applicants. In the end, I selected a hard-working young woman named Margaret "Gigi" McIntosh.

Gigi was on an upward trajectory in her career as an eventer, and I was happy to help her later gain a working student position with George and Monica Theodorescu in Germany. Gigi was showing great promise upon returning to the States, competing at the top levels of eventing, until a terrible fall resulted in a spinal cord injury that changed her life. It didn't surprise me one bit to learn she went on to become a dressage Paralympian at the 2016 Olympics in Rio. Talent is a gift, but it's nothing without determination, which Gigi always had in spades. I'm pleased to say we have remained lifelong friends.

With the help of all my working students during those years, I was able to continue to expand my business. What was particularly exciting was how my world began to overlap with riders and horses that would eventually be considered pioneers in the history of American dressage.

Edith Masters was one. Edith came soon after I settled into my new facility, and was the second person to offer me a horse to compete. That horse, Sergeant, was a semi-retired Grand Prix gelding who had been competed in Germany. I was quickly able to snag a United States Dressage Federation gold medal on Sergeant, which was considered a highly coveted achievement and an extra note of interest on my CV. Jessica Ransehousen continued faithfully with me, and from her family farm in New York, trailered in frequently with a couple of horses, usually before a competition. Sis, with her beautiful Thoroughbred mare Natu, also remained a consistent client. One day after a lesson, Sis was untacking her mare, and said with a smile, "You have no idea what I just did. I bought a little cabin on the river to be closer to you and Gladstone, and you are welcome to use it whenever you like!" Yet another amazingly generous offer that would become quite helpful later, in a way that would change my life. In the meantime, I continued to be spoilt for choice when it came to work.

I've always had a soft spot in my heart for off-the-track Thoroughbreds, or "OTTBs," and when Elizabeth Madlener, an aspiring Grand Prix rider from Washington, became a client of mine, a stream of them came through my barn. Elizabeth had two quite nice FEI Thoroughbreds, which had even caught the eye of Bengt Ljungquist at that year's US Equestrian Team (USET) Screening Trials for further training, held at Gladstone. Passionate about literature, Elizabeth chose names for her horses that are remembered to this day: Jonathan Swift and Gulliver's Travels.

As we were friends, Elizabeth came up with the idea of finding some nice OTTBs right off the track, which I would then purchase and pay to have shipped across the country to Long Valley, train, and sell. This proved to be both successful and profitable. I was flying high, and it seemed that somehow I had acquired a Midas touch.

Then something inexplicable happened.

I had been eager to reciprocate with business opportunities for my mentor Gunnar Andersen, after all the help he had given me in Denmark. And, to be honest, I was also eager for him to see how his ringing endorsement of me to Jessica was paying off. Not only had I scheduled a clinic for him at Long Valley, but I had mentioned him to the clinic organizers in California where I frequently taught; they, in turn, excitedly booked a subsequent clinic for Gunnar to teach on that side of the country, the next time he was scheduled to return to my place. As people knew he had worked with Jessica, the clinic at Long Valley successfully sold out, as higher-level riders trailered in from all over for the opportunity.

The trip to pick up my mentor from New York's Kennedy Airport was a tedious one: two and a half hours from Long Valley. This was not a truly big deal, but it did require tight scheduling around lessons and training.

Gerda was accompanying her husband on this three-week excursion, so Debbie and I made the drive to pick them up and brought them back to Long Valley to teach, and when it came time for their departure to California, we made the five-hour round-trip once again. During their stay in California, they were hosted by Kyra Downton, formerly of Russia, who evidently made a huge impression on them with her outstanding beef stroganoff. Their return from the San Francisco clinic obliged me to make the drive to Kennedy once again to bring Gunnar back for the second clinic at Long Valley, which had sold out yet again. You can imagine my reaction when I met Gunnar at the gate, only to hear the first words out of his mouth: "They have much better horses than you do."

I had no idea how to respond to that. How do you respond to that? "Oh, how nice for you?" "How refreshing it must have been for you to work with such quality?" "Thanks for the slap in the face with the wet herring?"

The statement was so unlike him that I didn't actually say anything, just gave a sort of crooked smile; I felt somewhat like a reprimanded son, especially on the way back to Long Valley. During the drive, much of the conversation morphed into a soliloquy on how wonderfully well he had been treated by the organizers in California—that he had been taken to the best restaurants, when he wasn't gorging on "the best beef stroganoff" he'd ever eaten. Never mind that Debbie and I had treated him and Gerda to very nice meals out, and more-than-comfortable accommodations. The unspoken sentiment that he hadn't been cared for nearly as well by me hung in the air. Had he found it necessary to take not only me down a peg, but the entire post?

Shaking it off, I returned with him to Long Valley, and of course the second clinic was a resounding success. So many auditors attended that, at the end, instead of pocketing the auditing fees as we normally would to pay the sizable electric bill, I impulsively offered Gunnar half as an unexpected bonus. My mistake was in mentioning what I was doing instead of just giving him the money; it later got back to me that when he returned to Denmark, while he waxed rhapsodic about how wonderfully he'd been treated in California, when it came to describing his clinic at Long Valley, he told all and sundry, "I had to pay half the electric bill!" I couldn't believe it—it felt like such a betrayal.

When July rolled around, my flummoxed emotions surrounding Gunnar faded, as America's most prestigious dressage show, Devon, was right around the corner. I remember it being hellishly hot, but there was a touch of pride in watching the brigade of horse trailers leaving my barn, on their way to Devon. To be at such a big show in the company of all these top riders, as well as coaching Jessica, felt pretty impressive and created quite a bit of notice. And with that notice came further possibilities.

Around this time, I received a call from a woman in Colorado named Trudi Peet. In 1971, she had purchased a Palomino Saddlebred/Thoroughbred cross named "Bit O'Shine," who was now in his teens and was up for sale. Would I take him on consignment to train and sell? I accepted the offer and, to be perfectly honest, didn't pay too much attention to the horse. He was suitable to let working students ride him, and while Trudi had mentioned that he'd been trained by Chuck Grant, considered to be "the father of American dressage," she had also said that the horse's training was somewhat "circus-y." After a couple of weeks, while the horse seemed very sweet and steady, I decided I'd better get going with him and got on.

Holy cow.

The moment I began to ride this horse, it was obvious that he could do everything perfectly. Everything. Push this button, and he piaffed and passaged. Push another button, and there were the one-tempi sequence changes. Humbled, I took my hat off to Chuck Grant. Bit O'Shine might have been limited in his gaits, but he was superb in the brain, and a true team player. I even gave George Morris a few lessons on him!

Not every horse, however, would have the talent to go on to Grand Prix glory. While I had several good prospects in training from all over the country, in order to pay the hefty monthly rent on Long Valley, I also took in anything and everything. Including a Saddlebred stallion: Rogue by name, and rogue by nature.

When you're in the business of training horses, it is not uncommon for owners to be less than forthcoming about a horse's faults. I have to say that in this case, that was not so. The owner—an exceedingly honest woman from Massachusetts—almost seemed to be trying to talk me out of taking him on. She stressed that Rogue was dangerous, and I have never had a horse arrive with such a list of dos and don'ts, before or since: "Don't do this or he will bite. Never do this or he will kick." He was also described as vicious in his stall, and I began wondering if I should approach the horse wearing a suit of armor. I will admit our first sessions were difficult, but over time I earned his respect. In fact, we reached a point where Rogue's training was going so well that I invited his owner to come watch him from the observation room above the arena.

She arrived with her mother, and I was surprised to see her leave the elderly woman in the car. I invited the mother in as well, and the owner looked at me, horrified. "She can't come into the barn or he'll go crazy," she said.

This, of course, sounded ridiculous, and I suggested she take her mother with her into the observation room.

"But he will see her through the glass!" she cried.

Lady, please, I thought.

I departed to tack up Rogue, and led him into the arena. As I was mounting, Rogue caught sight of "Mother" through the window, bolted, and crushed me into the wall. In my entire career, I have never experienced anything like that, and to this day I cannot explain it.

Nevertheless, I took a deep breath and got back on, and in the end, his owner was pleased with how he went. The result was that she left him with me for another six months of training.

As the year ebbed into August, I came home one evening to my apartment in Hackettstown, New Jersey, and found a message on my answering machine from Sis. Always happy to hear from her, I returned the call right away and she began to relay, with much excitement, a piece of news that would launch my career into overdrive.

CHAPTER
20

A BIG, BIG DEAL

"I HAVE EXCITING NEWS FOR YOU," Sis said, as soon as she picked up the line on the other end. "Have you heard of the show jumper Michael Matz? He's sponsored by F. Eugene Dixon, Jr, and his daughter, Ellin Dixon, wants to go into dressage." Sis then added, "They just bought Jet Run, and they also bought a Grand Prix dressage horse in Canada that was trained by Willy Schultheis. Anyway, their jumper trainer Jerry Baker just called me a few minutes ago because he's looking for a dressage trainer for this horse. Naturally, I thought of you—and if Mr. Dixon likes you, he will want you to train Ellin and this horse at Long Valley."

I thanked Sis for her vote of confidence and hung up. You might think me mad...in fact, looking back, I think I must have been mad, but in my defense, I was so busy during this time that the thought of training another horse was simply that—another horse. I was in no rush. Yes, being trained by Schultheis, Germany's legendary rider and trainer, was a big deal and spoke to the horse's quality, but my schedule was such that I would be riding my horses first thing the following morning, before driving two and a half hours to teach six lessons at a clinic at David and Patricia Goodman's Wonderland Farm. I'd stay overnight, and teach another six lessons before heading back to Long Valley. As the Dixons' place, Erdenheim Farm, was located in Springfield, Pennsylvania (four hundred and fifty acres, not far from the border of Philadelphia), I thought, *Okay, on my next trip to Wonderland, I'll make a side trip and see this horse at Erdenheim.* Which is exactly what I did.

Erdenheim is German for "earthly home." and the farm's origins go all the way back to 1765. It was magnificent, and even upon approaching it in my car, I was filled with awe.

Coming up to shake my hand and introduce himself was the jumper trainer, Jerry Baker, who was short of stature and built a bit like a fireplug. (I don't normally describe someone's features, but it's relevant to the rest of the story.) Jerry let me know that if Mr. Dixon liked me, they'd send the horse and Ellin to me for training. What was odd was that neither Mr. Dixon nor Ellin was there. Surely they wouldn't be making such a decision without meeting me personally. Was Ellin some privileged kid who couldn't be bothered to show up? It all felt a bit strange.

Jerry must have sensed my confusion, as he put in a call to Mr. Dixon to say I'd arrived and within minutes, Mr Dixon showed up, with his office manager and right-hand man Jack Albright. We stood around and chatted for a few minutes, and then, at my request, we stepped inside the barn to see the horse. Fruhwind was a striking black German Thoroughbred, beautifully put together, and he absolutely oozed quality.

"Okay, you wanna get on?" suggested Jerry.

Repeating the mantra used by pretty much every trainer, I firmly replied, "I'm not getting on until I see someone else ride him."

All eyes swung to Jerry.

"Hey," he protested, "I haven't ridden a horse in three years!" All eyes remained on him, unblinking, until he shrugged and said, "All right, I'll give it a go," and hoisted himself up into the saddle.

I don't know who was more uncomfortable, Jerry or the horse, but Jerry bounced around on an inverted and unhappy Fruhwind for a minute before I put a stop to his misery and got on. As soon as my feet were in the stirrups, I could feel how beautifully trained he was. Around we went, riding piaffe, passage, and a row of fifteen one-tempi changes. Mr. Dixon threw back his head and laughed, proclaiming, "Jerry gets on and it's awful; this guy gets on, and in two minutes, makes the horse look beautiful."

From there, the formalities were discussed. Mr. Dixon asked about Long Valley, and wanted to know more about it. Before an agreement was reached, Jerry said he'd like to come see the facility in person. This, of course, was to be expected; what I did not expect was for him to arrive by private jet instead of driving the two and a half hours to Long Valley by car.

After collecting Jerry from our local airport, we arrived at Long Valley. I gave him the full tour and showed him the large stall in which we'd house Fruhwind. He was comfortable enough to give me the thumbs up, and soon after, Ellin drove up for the first time. I was curious to see how this would go, to say the least.

All my judgments about her fell away as soon as we met and chatted. She politely explained that she had been away at school and had been unable to come earlier. She was courteous, down-to-earth, and modest. There was no precociousness or snobbery around her at all. I immediately felt very positive about how things would go, and go they did. After Fruhwind arrived, I was then sent another horse, Lynnewood Hall. Lynnewood Hall had no speed to match the collection of Dixon racehorses, nor did he show any talent as a jumper, so the thought was to "see if I could get any dressage out of him." And I could. Lynnewood Hall did actually have some talent, and he made it to Prix St Georges and Intermediare 1. Next came a small horse that Jerry thought might make a nice dressage mount for Ellin. So it seemed that in the blink of an eye, we had three horses, and with Bit O'Shine and Fruhwind, Ellin had two Grand Prix schoolmasters on which to learn.

Ellin proved quickly to be a serious and dedicated student, as she showed up, rain or shine, driving two hours each way five days a week. She soon purchased Bit O'Shine, giving the Dixons four horses at Long Valley, and she was progressing quickly. In late 1977, we found a schooling show nearby where she rode very well in her first Grand Prix. It turned out Lynnewood Hall was a bit tricky to ride, so I spent most of the time in his saddle, but he did make it to Intermediare 1, shortly before my old friend Raul de Leon bought him for a client.

Raul was an equitation trainer who had once trained Olympic gold medalist Tad Coffin. He had an amazing backstory. His family had fled Cuba during the Russian occupation, and, having seen Gunnar Andersen teach during the '60s at the Steinkraus stables, he had come to find me when he heard I had arrived in the same area, also teaching.

As my daybook bulged with appointments, I did find spare moments for a bit of a social life with fellow horse people who, like Raul, have remained lifelong friends to whom I'm much indebted.

Giving a clinic at Potomac Horse Center in Maryland led to my meeting and teaching Susan and James Katz. Their dedication included moving everything they had from Maryland to Long Valley and getting a house nearby just to work with me. To be on the receiving end of that sort of confidence is nothing short of humbling, and I'll always be grateful to them. After James passed, Susan remarried, and we are still in touch.

Also dear to my heart was a German immigrant named Jutta Griffith, and her husband John. Jutta had a modest "backyard" type of horse, and after taking some lessons, she and John would invite me, as well as George Morris, over to their gorgeous home for lunch. She, like Sis, had a big heart and simply enjoyed doing kind things for me, including wonderful Thanksgiving dinners and even taking me to Manhattan to show me around. It was with Jutta that I had my first taste of the kind of Japanese restaurant where the chefs throw knives. These sorts of outings led to my becoming crazy about New York, and Jutta, who called herself my "American mother," really became that. She was blonde, funny and an incredible cook, and her house became like a second home to me.

Meanwhile, it became apparent that there wasn't another minute that could be squeezed from my schedule to ride any more horses. Instead of adding any more lessons, I came up with the idea of renting out a block of stalls for boarding horses. Thank God Debbie continued to prove herself to be a terrific stable manager; to my regret, her Thoroughbred was so hot-headed that he proved difficult to train. What I was able to offer her, though, was the opportunity to ride other horses and teach other lower-level students, and this she did admirably. Her putting an ad in *The Chronicle* led to my being able to rent out those stalls to Chris Kelley, a hunter-jumper and equitation trainer who took all six.

My relationship with Edith Masters continued to grow, and out of the blue, as October rolled around, Sis asked if Edith and I would ride in a dressage exhibition at Madison Square Garden. Edith agreed to ride her dark mare, La Paloma, while Mr. Dixon gave me permission to use Fruhwind.

There was nothing bigger than "the Garden" in those days, and to say I was nervous as hell put it mildly. We moved both horses to the Steinkraus estate, where we worked with Michael Handler, the son of the late director of the Spanish Riding School, Col. Hans Handler. Michael had come over to become a trainer, and was a well-known judge. We were grateful to have him put together a pas-de-deux for us.

Two days before the big night, we practiced our routine in the Steinkraus arena. I had sent my tailcoat to the dry cleaner a couple of days before, and had instructed a working student to pick it up. This she did, but she left it in the back of her station wagon with the windows rolled down as she ran a couple of other errands. Needless to say, by the time she returned—no coat. All I could think was there was some guy wandering around 42nd Street in a beautifully tailored, wool tailcoat with yellow vest points.

In the meantime, I panicked. What on earth was I to do? Sis came to the rescue—and this is embarrassing—by giving me her tailcoat to borrow. I was actually skinny enough to wear it, although the vest points were too low and I had to hope no one would notice the buttons were on the "wrong" side. I was put up at the Pennsylvania Hotel across the street from the Garden, and on the big night, I was so anxious I couldn't eat a thing.

It was a big, big deal, and anyone who was anyone was there. I just wanted to go get my horse, but was obliged to glad-hand and chit-chat beforehand. George Morris introduced me to Paul Newman, because George taught Paul's daughter. Knowing such celebrities were in the audience did nothing to settle the butterflies in my stomach! However, as Edith and I finally entered the darkened arena and the spotlight illuminated us and our horses, my nerves vanished, and I was in my element. Confidently, we did everything from the Grand Prix; we performed half-pass zig-zags, and then Edith piaffed in the center of the arena while I passaged around her. The horses couldn't have been more different. While La Paloma was a Hanoverian, "The Dove" actually moved like a sewing machine, and Fruhwind, a Thoroughbred, had huge, expressive flying changes. Despite the fact that their color was the only thing they had in common, both horses behaved beautifully, and I was so overcome with joy (and relief!) that as the audience erupted into applause, which turned into a standing ovation, I swept off my top hat in a flourish of grateful acknowledgment.

Edith, however, would bring me back to earth immediately with a glacial expression and a stinging rebuke.

"You could have told me you were going to take your hat off," she snapped as we rode out of the arena. "I would have saluted."

CHAPTER
21

DANISH WEDDING

KEEPING MY WORD THAT I WOULD RETURN regularly to teach clinics, I made the drive back to Plattsburgh in soft, autumnal light. At the end of the day–actually, well into the night–I was catching up with John, as we sat in the lodge before a crackling fire and talked about the recent events of our lives. It had been a beautiful day, and in the clear November sky, there was a spectacular sunset, when it suddenly occurred to me that, while John was a good friend, I was hanging out with him because there was no one I cared for waiting for me to return home. The realization hit me like a ton of bricks: I missed Birgit. Despite having gone our separate ways and having little contact over the past two years, I never stopped having deep feelings toward her.

My career had grown more than I could have imagined when I first arrived in the States, and while there had been great success, at the end of the day, there was really no one with whom I could share those triumphs–as well as the disappointments–who knew me as well as Birgit. Impulsively, I asked John if I could use his phone, knowing it would be early morning in Denmark when I called her–which was probably the only time during the day when I could catch her. Clearly, she was somewhat surprised to hear from me, and after exchanging pleasantries for a couple of minutes, I plunged ahead and asked, "Would you like to come over for Christmas?"

I can't imagine what her expression might have been, on the other end of the line, but in her typical understated manner, she hesitated for a few moments, then replied, "I haven't been thinking of that."

I waited her out. While I secretly felt that I was finally ready for a commitment, I didn't dare let on, mostly because I was worried that after two years with barely a "hello," she might say, "Huh. That's nice for you."

I don't think I exhaled until Birgit finally agreed, and as the holidays rolled around, she flew over to visit—after telling all our mutual friends who knew we'd broken up that she was going on a ski trip in Austria. She didn't want anyone to know, and I could understand that.

Upon her arrival, I picked her up at Kennedy and was pleased to see she had followed my suggestion to bring riding clothes, as there would be ample opportunity to ride some nice horses. Frank Chapot had sent me a horse to sell which wasn't much of a dressage prospect, but Birgit took him over some big jumps, and rode a few other horses as well. My working relationship with Ellin was developing in a really positive way, and through her, I made arrangements to take Birgit to the Dixon farm to watch Michael Matz ride—not on Jet Run, but other great horses he had at the time. I wanted Birgit to see Erdenheim Farm, as I had an idea I'd put on the back burner that had now come to fruition.

Birgit and I spent a lovely Christmas together and rode together, and I finally took advantage of Sis's offer to use her cabin on the river. We had an unforgettable New Year's Eve dinner with George Morris and his assistant Kathy Moore at Hunterdon Farm. Sometime during the evening, we made a deal that I would give Kathy a dressage lesson in exchange for George giving Birgit a lesson.

Too soon, it seemed, I drove Birgit back to Kennedy Airport to return to Denmark, in early January. Directly afterward, in February, I returned to Denmark as well—my "official" reason was to visit my parents, and I actually was at my parents' home when Birgit swung by to visit one Saturday afternoon. The timing was perfect: I took her to the beach—Tomaj Beach—where my father had always taken the orphans from the children's home, and I proposed. It wasn't an impulsive proposal. I was prepared. It came, however, in two parts, the latter being non-negotiable: "Will you marry me? Will you move to the United States?"

This was a big risk, but after rekindling our relationship, I had no doubt she would say yes. What I didn't realize was that she would have a caveat of her own. "Yes," she replied, then added, "But only if both my horses can come." Game, set, and match.

We told my family members, who were overjoyed—I remember my mother leaping up from her chair with excitement—then drove downtown to get a bottle of champagne before sharing the news with Birgit's family; they were also delighted. Immediately, we sat down with our respective schedules to choose a date for the wedding. Only horse people will try to fit in something as momentous as a wedding somewhere in between teaching clinics and horse shows. And the only day we both had open was April 1st—an easy date to remember, but only two months away.

We knew of a nice place on the coast, Hotel Marina, for our guests to stay. Together we drew up the guest list, and were pleased that my cousin's husband—who, late in life, became a priest—got permission to preside over the ceremony. Birgit's hometown of Horsholm had a beautiful old church that would accommodate us as well as our seventy-five guests. We decided to make it a black tie affair where people would meet at the church.

Weeks later, following traditional protocol, I flew in early and stayed in Birgit's apartment the night before the wedding, while she stayed with her parents. On the big day, I walked up the aisle alongside my father in my rented tuxedo, and then Birgit came up on the arm of her father. I was delighted she had chosen to wear a hat—I had thought she would look lovely in a hat—and she carried a bouquet of roses and baby's breath. Solemnly, we exchanged vows.

Nothing, absolutely nothing, had prepared us for the sight that greeted us as we walked out of the church together. Arranged by our friends, a carriage to which was harnessed four bay horses waited for us, and behind the carriage were sixteen riders, all in red jackets, on impeccably turned-out mounts. It was a complete shock, and the memory of us traveling in that carriage, through the alley of trees that framed the church on either side, with water views beyond that, is as vivid to me today as if it had happened yesterday. The carriage wound its way through the forest toward Hotel Marina, with our guests following behind in their own cars, and while it was indeed a cold day, our hearts and clasped hands were warm.

Danish weddings are great fun but also can feel endless. Especially on hard-backed chairs! When we arrived at the hotel, all the wedding gifts were on display, and the celebratory reception awaited us. Tradition dictates that speeches are to be given by everyone: the bride's father, my parents, then further family members, friends, assorted dogs, and anyone we happened to pass on the street in the last decade. In all seriousness, I was delighted to have Gunnar Andersen sitting close to my family, as he was very special to me. I was rather looking forward to what he had to say. While he knew Birgit as a show jumper and spoke a few complimentary words about her, when he got to me, I sat up and turned kind, expectant eyes toward him. My mentor's prepared remarks began with his having enjoyed teaching me each Wednesday for the past six years, and how much I had improved in my riding. He went on to wish us good luck "in the big USA," where he knew so many people. Then, instead of a funny story or anything particularly touching, he simply said, "Gunnar has always been a nice, polite young man. Thank you." And he sat down.

Luckily, Nis Valdemar got the party atmosphere going by standing up and reminding me of embarrassing times at Flensburg: "You remember Rehbein, right, and the straw bales?" After this, songs were turned into parodies, featuring our names and funny memories.

When it was my turn to make a speech, while my mother thought it was rather impersonal, Birgit understood when I said, "What I have to tell you, I'll say when we're on our own."

After four hours, the dinner was over, and the dancing began, to the music of a band which later played the traditional bride and groom's waltz. With all the guests standing around us in a circle, clapping their hands, we danced—and Gunnar Andersen must have had a cognac or two, as he became quite boisterous during our waltz, yelling, "More impulsion!"

Finally, we made the dash through handfuls of thrown rice into Birgit's blue Volkswagen Beetle, adorned with the obligatory tin cans tied to the bumper, and set off for an old inn next to Castle Fredensborg. The queen of Denmark spent her summers in that castle, and the inn not only had a fantastic menu, but was set within a very pretty landscape. We really had no time after the wedding to catch our breath, as the very next day we had to get together with our parents and arrange to ship the horses to the United States.

Birgit decided to keep a journal of all our adventures, titled, "The Journey to America," all written in Danish—and it has been most useful in chronicling what transpired.

On April 6th, we made our first attempt to leave for the States with the horses, in addition to a sizable load in the Beetle. We arrived at the stable in Lundegaard, and Birgit longed both Veronica and Sharoh for twenty minutes before wrapping their legs and loading them up. As soon as they were loaded, they were sedated, and the biggest horse transport company in Denmark, Gunnar's Horse Transportation, departed with them onboard and us in pursuit, after we said our goodbyes to friends and students, who had even filmed and interviewed us for fun before our departure.

Our next stop was the shipping office near the airport, to collect all the required paperwork. Gunnar went in with the agent, then came out wearing an expression that Birgit, in her Danish notes, described as, "looking completely wrong in the face." We immediately knew the news wasn't good. At all.

As it happened, our plane had broken down, and we were stuck. What else could we do, we thought, except drive to the airport anyway and try to negotiate? We spoke with people in the freight area—all very nice—with our horses still standing quietly in the van. When word got out to our friends, they began to show up, kindly bringing coffee. Or at least most of them did; leave it to Ina Zetterstrom and her boyfriend to bring gin and tonic instead, which we gratefully received. Then another fifteen or so people arrived, and more of Birgit's family—everyone hanging out at the airport created something of an impromptu "bon voyage" party.

After quite some time, an airport official came out to say we could leave the next morning at four in the morning—20 hours later. This meant phoning Lundegaard to see if we could board the two horses for the night. Our "Journey to America" was turning into a nightmare, and our good friend Tommy couldn't resist looking at Birgit when we arrived back at the stable, and saying, "I told you not to believe that Gunnar was going to take you to America!"

There was nothing to do but keep moving forward. With some friends in tow, we had dinner at a restaurant called The Spanish Grill, then tried to get a bit of shut-eye, as we had to be up at nine in the evening to get ready for our early-morning departure. At midnight, we left with the horses, who really must have wondered what the hell was going on, having had to wrap and sedate them once again.

This time, we succeeded, and immediately went out to the cargo area with the horse van. The horses were able to go directly from the van into their shipping stalls, which were pushed up into the belly of the plane. It goes without saying that these were not the days of flying horses all over the world, as is done today. This was quite new in Denmark and both Sharoh—whose nickname was *"Rott"* (Danish for "Rat")—and Veronica were well behaved.

Veronica could jump the moon, but, oddly, with no bascule. She was flat-backed, very hot, and hyper on the ground. As tense as she was, it was decided she needed another dose of "Schnapps," but she was clever; she hid it in her mouth, and then spit it out. We were told we would have a "specialist" who was going to fly with the horses. What we got was a fellow named Frederiksen, who had taken a crash course about how to fly with horses, although he knew nothing about them; the one thing he did know was how to shoot one in the head with a rifle, should they panic on the plane. This was the way things were. We could see that Rott was beginning to become bug-eyed, so he had an extra shot of "Schnapps" as well. By 4:15, we were finally loaded on the plane with all our gear. The horses raised their heads, looking out of their crates, but remained relatively quiet. We stood at their heads as the plane roared down the runway, and the next thing we knew we were in the air.

We could now relax, and I made a nice bed on hay bales, with newspapers and a blanket. Birgit had three seats on which to lie, behind the three pilots. We had a long flight ahead of us, and were supposed to land in Montreal to pick up more cargo before reaching our destination at Kennedy.

It might have been the pressure as we began to descend, or the roar of the engines, but Sharoh began to panic, and we realized we were too late to give him another round of sedation. He was out of control, repeatedly throwing himself around inside his stall and even flinging himself on the ground. Frederiksen reached for his rifle...

Birgit and I, hiding our own panic, were trying to hold onto the horse, and we shook his halter violently, trying to make him stand up and stand still. It worked, and we were able to top off his sedation, so that we could land in Montreal and the horses would still be relaxed when we went back into the air within the hour.

I had precious few minutes to dash from the plane to call Long Valley and confirm all was fine, and that Kris Kelley was going to pick us up. As we taxied for take-off to New York, Rott had another nervous breakdown and went nuts inside his crate. Frederiksen once again reached for his rifle, and we implored him not to. He called the captain, who said, "I'll give you five minutes and that's it." Having this ultimatum was nothing we'd ever planned for, and all we could do was continue shaking his halter to make him stand. Each moment was terrifying, and with one minute to spare, talking quietly and stroking him, we finally got him quiet, and we were in the air. This time, we knew what to expect on the descent, and again he had more "Schnapps."

We could have kissed the ground when we landed. Airport crew streamed in, including cleaners to collect hay in plastic bags, and a vet. Finally, the horses in their crates were rolled out onto American soil. The horses were then sent—still in their shipping stalls—to Cliffton, New Jersey, for the required three days of quarantine.

Everything went very fast after that. Birgit got her green card, we flew through immigration, and Kris picked us up in his truck. Sitting amongst all our luggage, exhausted, we drank champagne from a bottle he had brought. And once the horses were safely tucked away in Long Valley, Birgit and I boarded another plane—this time, to our week-long honeymoon in Barbados.

We still have Birgit's "Journey to America" journal, with her typically succinct remarks describing our traveling ordeal:

"There's no refusal now, Rott Daddy! Finally, we landed. Whew. NO FUN."

CHAPTER
22

ERDENHEIM

T WAS THE TWO VISITS I HAD MADE to the Dixons' farm, Erden- heim, that had sparked an idea that began to flit within my brain well before Christmas, and well before my proposal to Birgit. Birgit, of course, had seen the place; I'd taken her there when she came to watch Michael Matz ride, and she had been duly impressed. But it had been during my first visit, with Sis, that I had noticed how empty the stable was. This huge building stood with twenty stalls surrounded by an indoor galloping track—the size was unbelievable—and that is what gave me the idea. And so, one raw winter's day, after working all four of Ellin's horses but before she made her daily two-hour trek home, I took her into my office. We didn't even sit down.

"I have this wild idea I want to throw at you," I began. "There's no rush to decide, and if you'd rather not, it's fine. But what would you and your family think if I came and trained you at Erdenheim?"

Ellin thought for a moment, then said she'd discuss it with her father. I didn't expect anything less.

When I saw her two days later, she said, "My father would like to talk to you about relocating."

As much as I would have liked to take a meeting immediately, I was booked solid with teaching, both at Long Valley and at clinics, and therefore I had no time to make the four-hour round trip to Erdenheim. Clearly, Ellin's parents assumed I would—who wouldn't?—because one Saturday morning, they arrived unexpectedly.

"If you won't come to the boss," said Mrs. Dixon, stepping out of the car and smiling, "we will bring the boss to you."

They watched me teach, and afterwards, we went to eat at The Public House near Gladstone, New Jersey. During the course of the meal, we agreed on salary and my remaining an independent contractor, and, very importantly, we arranged for me to have four stalls for boarding and training my personal horses. Since Erdenheim was a private farm—his farm—I felt Mr. Dixon was extremely generous in allowing me to bring in Susan and James Katz, and their three horses. Lastly, knowing Ellin's ambitions and that she had her parents' full support in her dressage career, I asked whether they would be willing to let me go to Europe to look for more horses for her, as well as some to train. Mr. Dixon readily agreed, although Mrs. Dixon hesitated a couple of moments before replying, "Well, we started with a pony..." which brought a hearty laugh to the table, as they recalled Ellin's early years in the saddle.

I had been at Long Valley for over a year, and it wouldn't be until June 1st that I would move to Erdenheim. Ellin would no longer have to spend literally twenty hours a week commuting back and forth, and I was out from under the monthly rent and added responsibility that came with leasing Long Valley. But best of all, Erdenheim represented an exciting new chapter for Birgit and me as we began our life together.

And when we returned from our island honeymoon, tanned and eager to get to work, we immediately began preparing for our move to Erdenheim. There were all the logistics to consider: loading up tack, supplies, and equipment, not to mention a string of horses. I immediately realized what life at Erdenheim held in store for us when, a few days before our move on June 1st, farm manager Stan Gates, like a genie snapping his fingers, telephoned to say that two horse vans would be sent from Erdenheim to pick up both Ellin and Birgit's horses, as well as all our equipment.

The Erdenheim "halo" seemed to follow us when Birgit and I decided to rent an apartment in Flourtown, within a characterful Victorian building, just one mile from Erdenheim. As soon as the landlord realized I was training the Dixons' daughter, the apartment was ours, with no background check or deposit required.

What was particularly nice for our three Long Valley working students who followed me—one being our longtime friend Margaret McIntosh—was that their lives, too, would change for the better. At Erden-heim, not only were they given good salaries and lovely living quarters just a few yards from the barn, but each girl was responsible for only three horses. Pretty much a dream job for any working student!

With the arrival of August, I approached Mr. Dixon about a buy-ing trip to Europe, and he agreed. I have to say that that first trip was one of the best—if not the best—trip I ever took. Obviously, I went to Denmark, which meant I could see my parents as well; then I headed straight to my old haunt, Frederiksdal. One of my former students, Irene—the same Irene who had kindly arranged the champagne toast on my flight to America—had a super young horse with terrific hind legs named Gin, whom she had developed to 4th Level. Once in the saddle, I could tell he needed a little work, but his talent was obvious. I immediately called Mr. Dixon to report I'd found a great prospect, and was given the green light to have him vetted by our own Dr. Allen Leslie, and then purchased.

The next stop was a riding facility 45 minutes north of Copenha-gen, Barthahus, where I met Ulla Petersen. Ulla had a record which boasted accomplishments such as being named Danish National Champion five times, as well as finishing 5th at the European Cham-pionships on her Grand Prix horse Chigwell. Now 15, Chigwell would be the perfect competitive schoolmaster for Ellin.

We—and pretty much the entire European dressage community—were well aware of his reputation to buck here or there during a test. He didn't do it consistently, but no one knew when or why this love-ly English Thoroughbred would feel the need to give his opinion. In fact, Chigwell was the only horse that was given a double-page photo spread in Harry Boldt's *Das Dressurpferd*, showing him giving one of his famous kicks.

Ellin flew over, accompanied by Dr. Lesley, who went over both horses with a fine-toothed comb, and the purchases were made. It was decided we should have a celebratory lunch to toast our new horses at Tivoli, where I introduced them to Danish Schnapps, "Akvavit" or "Aqua Vitae" ("The Water of Life"). This traditional drink tastes quite a bit like gin, but contains all sorts of botanicals—cumin, dill, and even amber—that give it a pine-like taste. Ellin wrinkled her nose, not caring for it at all, but when we all agreed that no one liked the name of her new horse Gin, she looked at the label on the golden bottle of Akvavit, which read, Jubilaeum, and then and there, he was given a far more appropriate moniker.

With a lot of dedication and hard work from us both, Ellin later began to reap the rewards. In 1982, in Lausanne, Switzerland, she represented the United States. with Jubi, as the only American rider competing in the small tour (the Prix St Georges and Intermediare 1) at the World Championships. Afterwards, I took over the ride to develop the horse to Grand Prix the following year. With Ellin back in the saddle when Jubi was fully confirmed at top level, they had great success, and even finished 5th in the selection trials for the 1984 Olympic Games in Los Angeles.

On Chigwell, Ellin bagged the National U.S. Grand Prix Championship in 1981, and went on to win several Grand Prix classes. In fact, the only time Ellin didn't win was when Chigwell kicked out, but upon coming to America, he gave his rear "salute" less and less.

The Dixons were wonderful to all their retired horses and gave them lovely "forever" homes. These horses had their own special barn with one employee to care for them all—including the show jumpers and one of Ellin's first ponies, who was probably 40 years old. It was decided that Chigwell, having campaigned so long and so successfully, would be the newest resident of that glorious "assisted living" facility, but sadly, on his way home from his last show, at age 20, he suffered colic and we lost him. He was a very special horse to me, and I'll never forget his generous nature.

Me, Beth Tait, and Chuck Grant, during my visit to see Chuck and Mari Zudunic, in Michigan. This was taken in 1980, when I was a guest instructor at the USDF Trainer Seminar.

Birgit's and my first Vermont Christmas in 1981, in our barely finished log cabin.

Me, Birgit, and my mentor Gunnar Andersen in 1981, during our first Florida season; we are at Howard and Gisela Pferdekamper's Hannover Farm in Indiantown, Florida.

UNITED STATES EQUESTRIAN TEAM, INC.

Gladstone, New Jersey 07934
(201) 234-1251

292 Bridge Street, South Hamilton, Massachusetts 01982
(617) 468-7377

20 March 1982

To Whom it May Concern:

    I am delighted to offer this reference in support of Mr. Gunnar Ostergaard's application to become a citizen of the United States. I have had frequent contact with Mr. Ostergaard during the past five years, having known of him by reputation for a much longer period through his teacher, Gunnar Andersson, a friend of long standing. I have found him to be a person of outstanding integrity, industry and ability, and can affirm that he has earned a fine reputation both as a person and as one of the most sought-after dressage trainer/riders in the country.

    I have no hesitancy whatever in urging favorable consideration of Mr. Ostergaard's application. He will be a real asset to our country.

William C. Steinkraus
President

WCS:hs

Contributions are deductible for federal income tax purposes

I am still proud of this letter of reference from the legendary
William C. Steinkraus.

A mock wedding during the 1981 season, held in Wildwood, Florida—with Anne Gribbons serving as the "priest." My cousin Hanne and I still laugh about these photos when we get together in Denmark.

The USET cordially invites you for
cocktails and a buffet dinner
with the Three Day Event riders in training
with Gunnar Østergaard
in the Trophy Room at the USET Training Center
on Tuesday, February 10, 1987
at 6:30 p.m.

DRESS: Casual   RSVP: 201-234-1251

I always enjoyed working with USET team riders, and three-day event riders, in general.

Jubilaum was one of the first horses I imported for the Dixon family. He received many scores of "10" for his extended trot, including from international judges when he won at Devon and other major shows. *Photo by Mary Phelps*

Ellin Dixon had great success with Fruhwind, one of her early FEI horses.
Photo by Mary Phelps

A 10-year student/ trainer relationship in dressage was as rare then as it is today. When Ellin and I parted ways, we decided to have a party. This is how we ended up.

Gibraltar was trained by the legendary Willi Schultheis. What an honor it was to continue training this great horse under the Dixon family ownership.

Birgit at Devon, on our Trakehner Grand Prix stallion Elbiskus.
Photo by Terri Miller

We had so much fun with the Steiners—Betsy and her then-husband Uwe—at horse shows. Here, Betsy and I are about to take off.

We enjoyed such good times with Fred (right) and Peggy (mounted) Fürth, who bought the Grand Prix horse Hadrian from us. At left is John Charleborough, with his family.

I'm on Peggy Fürth's horse Hadrian in 1987, at an exhibition— "Dressage in the Wine Country"—in Santa Rosa, California.
Photo by MJ Wickham Photography

Nightwatch, a great horse owned by Lynn Sheehan, had his own opinion about participating in a clinic with German master Harry Boldt.

General Jack Burton was a great contributor to US equestrian sport; I feel privileged to have known him.

It was an honor to serve on USET committees for several years, and Olympic gold medalist Tad Coffin and his mentors Raul de Leon, Bert de Nemethy, and Jack LeGoff, put me in good company on the Westmoreland Davis advisory council.

Looks like Birgit and I were having a serious talk at Devon.

Riding Elektron at Erdenheim Farm. This stallion had a successful breeding career after his dressage days were over.

Birgit and I bought 245 acres in Chester, Vermont, in 1981, and enjoyed this view from our log-and-stone home for almost 40 years. We designed our mountain home ourselves, and built it over several years. We loved it.

We brought horses to our native Denmark in the summer of 1992. We enjoyed some good wins and international placings in Sweden and Belgium—here I am at the top of the podium.

PRIX ST. GEORGES HORSE OF THE YEAR

Lutece

STATISTICS

1984
Bay
16.2
Danish
Gelding

Sire: Alexander
Dam: Mare by Soloist

High Score:
71.316

Rider:
Gunnar
Ostergaard,
Chester, VT

Owner:
Gunnar
Ostergaard &
Louise Woodruff,
Binghamton, NY

Trainer, rider and part-owner Gunnar Ostergaard, thinks Lutece (pronounced "Lutess") has the 'right stuff' to make a very promising Grand Prix horse. The nine year old Danish gelding is "unusually good behind," Ostergaard said. "He has a good engine and wonderful expression" – two hallmarks of an international horse.

Ostergaard and his wife, Brigit, bought the gelding in Denmark as a two and one-half year old bargain, leaving him there until they were sure he was maturing as they had suspected he would. Lutece was started in Denmark by a colleague of Ostergaard's and then arrived in the U.S. at five.

"He got kind of a late start," Ostergaard admitted, but handling the importation in this fashion, they knew they had a horse full promise. They share this rising star with good family friends, Dr. and Mrs. Woodruff, as half-owners.

Brigit Ostergaard showed the gelding briefly at First Level. Then Lutece stayed home, learning his lessons before coming back to competition at Fourth Level and Prix St. Georges.

"He had a little bit of trouble learning his changes," said Ostergaard, "but that's all behind them now. With an "extremely

Photo: Mary Phelps

The horse Lutece, in 1993; he may have been the most talented horse Birgit and I have owned. *Photo by Mary Phelps*

Lutece winning at Devon in 1993.
Photo by Mary Phelps

Birgit on Tanzkönig, owned by Priscilla Endicott.

I do believe a few cruise ship vacations were both needed and deserved.

We had so many great times with Pat and Mary Anne O'Connor—Pat was my best male friend.

Escada, owned by Jean and Nick Vinios of Massachusetts, was the USDF I1 Horse of the Year in 1994.
Photo by Mary Phelps

Robby winning the Grand Prix at Devon. This horse may have had the best mind of any horse I have worked with. *Photo by Terri Miller*

Birgit, during our arrival at the airport in Honolulu, Hawaii, for 10 days of teaching. A nice place to be invited to work.

Admiron was Birgit's best Grand Prix horse. Here he was at the beautiful King Oaks Farm in Massachusetts, which was owned by our dear friends Fran and Tom Cross. *Photo by Hoof Pix Sport Horse Photography*

We bought our training facility just outside Chester, Vermont, in 1993, right after returning from our summer in Denmark.

Some of our best years were spent between summers in Vermont and our Ocala farm, with its beautiful live oak trees, in the winter. *Photo by Jenna Dominick*

Andromeda, owned by Mrs. Nornie Loving of Ohio, was National Grand Prix Vintage Cup Champion in 1997.

Annie Morris and I had a great working relationship for well over a decade—and a continuing friendship. Annie bought Waldemar from us as a five-year-old; here he is during the Grand Prix competition at the Festival of Champions at Gladstone.

The invitation we sent out to friends and neighbors for my fiftieth birthday, and a portrait of me and Birgit at the party.

On May 16, 1996 12:30 p.m.
please come
UP THE HILL
TO DEERWOOD FARM
(NOT OVER THE HILL)
TO CELEBRATE MY 50TH BIRTHDAY

Birgit and I would like to invite you
to a luncheon and a fun afternoon.

RSVP by April 25   Florida 407-844-3069 til 4/10
                         Vermont 802-875-4186

Dinner

Ahi Tuna Sashimi With Avocado
Served with Banana Ketchup
Georges Duboeuf Chardonnay, 2001

Roast Strip Loin of Veal
Linguini in Truffle Cream Sauce
Chateau de L'Isolette Cotes de Luberon, 1998

Chilled Rhubarb Soup with Mint
and Marzipan Savarin with Berries
Sauternes J. J. Mortier, 1999

Birgitte Federspiel, wife of Ulrik Federspiel—who was at that time the ambassador from Denmark in the United States—was a student in my Maryland clinics. This was a small dinner party at the Royal Danish Embassy held in my honor. An unforgettable experience.

Wynsome, owned by Debbie Hamilton, found Grand Prix success, and even won a CDI Grand Prix... on days where he did not spook.

Due to unfortunate circumstances, I was never able to bring the talented Donzetti to his full potential.

Our dearest friend, Ellen Holm McKee, whom I met in Denmark. She helped me make my first US contacts. She died at 92 on her and her husband Bill's ranch in Wyoming. Here she is with Birgit.

Birgit's Danish Grand Prix Jumper champion Sharoh retired to Ellen McKee's farm in Maryland where he lived to be 31.

Chopping wood
by hand has
always been a
relaxing chore
for me.

A great photo of my mentor
Gunnar Andersen; he kept that
pipe in place all the time, even
when doing world-class piaffe.

I loved Monhegan; I called him my "best
time of the day" horse, and with him, both
riding and apple time were a pleasure.
He was National Grand Prix Vintage Cup
champion in 2010 and 2012.

Our farm in Denmark; we moved there part-time in 2014. In these you can see a view of the farmland, as well as my favorite place on the farm—I love to work around the banks of our pond.

On the balcony of our condo in the 1990s, overlooking the Atlantic Ocean in Singer Island, Florida. *Photo by Janne Bugrtup*

CHAPTER
23

A HORSE, A DOG, AND A FARM

WITH FRUHWIND, CHIGWELL, AND BIT O'SHINE making up the string of Grand Prix horses for Ellin, it was clear we were going to be working together for a long time. Keeping this in mind, I began to embark on the other passion in my life, which began at the age of 12, eavesdropping on my parents from the back seat of our car, and continues to this day: real estate.

Contentedly ensconced at Erdenheim, I mentioned to Mrs. Dixon one morning that Birgit and I would like to look for our own farm in the vicinity, creating a permanent base. Perhaps she recognized my work ethic and willingness to do what it took to get a job done; nevertheless, once again, the Dixon generosity blew me away when she replied without hesitation, "I'm sure my husband would co-sign the mortgage for you."

Birgit and I share a similar taste in homes: we both have a fondness for rustic, stone-built houses. And in Pennsylvania, there were scores of them. But finding one that would be within driving distance of Erdenheim would take some looking. Knowing that with the Dixons' guarantee there would be no difficulty securing a mortgage, I began looking nonstop—like a man possessed. While Birgit would scour the classified ads in the paper and reject a house by its description, I simply had to see for myself, and spent precious days off driving endless miles only to realize she'd been right. We had a shopping list of requirements: the house must have either existing riding facilities or land suitable to easily build them. There would have to be relatively level turnout, and a flat area that would require minimum grading to create an arena. And, most of all, it couldn't be more than a 50-minute drive.

During that summer of 1978, we must have viewed a hundred farms, and still hadn't found what we were looking for. We weren't losing hope–far from it–but it was frustrating to want something very much that just didn't seem to be in the cards. It wouldn't be until the following year that our luck would change.

With Birgit's birthday looming, she was planning a return trip to Denmark in June to visit family and friends. And just before she left, on the 10th, I said, "Since you won't be here on your actual birthday, what is your birthday wish?"

Having made the switch from jumping to dressage, she quipped, "A horse, a dog and a farm."

Shortly after she departed, I happened upon an ad describing a farm in Quakertown, Pennsylvania: a small, two-story stone house on 29 acres, with an old-fashioned Pennsylvania "bank" barn. This was a style of barn with a bank on one side that made for an easy entry into the enormous hayloft, which hulked over the stalls beneath. I had to look. If my car had been fitted with rocket boosters, I would have deployed them.

I was smitten. The house was indeed small, but had lovely sash windows set within its Pennsylvania "red stone" that let in a lot of light, and was positioned in a pretty courtyard, embraced by charming stone walls. The sprawling acreage was a mixture of woods and grass fields, and was beautifully secluded. In fact, it was a mere two miles from Lake Nockamixon State Park. The only downside was that the barn was simply too primitive and wouldn't work for us, but the potential was there to redo it. And it too was surrounded by stone walls. For me, this was it.

As soon as I returned to our apartment, I phoned Birgit in Denmark–funny how the two most important calls I've ever made to her were when we were oceans apart.

"I think I've found our farm," I said, trying to temper the excitement I was feeling. "It's a 40-minute drive to Erdenheim." Pausing, I closed my eyes tightly shut and crossed my fingers before adding, "I guess we have to wait until you get back and hope it's still available."

What you must realize about Birgit and me and our long, happy marriage is that we've never been a "honey, sugar, sweetie" sort of couple. We're not gooey. We have always had, besides obvious affection, great mutual respect for one another. So when Birgit softly replied, "Go ahead, baby," I nearly fell over. Bursting with excitement, I thanked her for her belief in my find, and wasn't at all surprised that it was love at first sight when she returned.

In those days, closings took forever, and after sitting and signing towers of paper for two hours, I can still remember the feeling of heady excitement when we turned into the driveway of our first "Deerwood Farm," knowing it was finally ours. We had bought a bottle of champagne, which we sipped on the back porch, still trying to wrap our heads around the fact that we now owned our first farm.

Immediately we set about tearing out the small existing stalls and replacing them with five larger ones, as well as a tack room and feed room. An added bonus to the property was a tiny stone guest house which would serve well to accommodate a working student. It felt like kismet when around that time, Laurie Stanton, a young woman whom I'd met teaching clinics in Syracuse, wrote us a very touching letter saying that her greatest dream would be to become a working student for us and bring her horse. Without hesitation, we invited her, and she moved into the tiny guest house, while her horse took up residence in one of our five stalls.

Meanwhile, the main house needed a fair bit of modernizing. We tore down the plaster wall in the kitchen to reveal the original stonework behind it. We tidied up the little living room past the stairs, which had its own fireplace. It still makes me laugh to remember that upon entering the dining room, there was a wooden screen standing off to one side. We didn't think anything of it, and never thought to look behind it until the place was ours, at which point further inspection revealed a toilet! We later learned that this home had been leased to a gentleman in a wheelchair, and obviously he hadn't been able to use the bathroom upstairs. That bathroom was tiny, and could only hold a shower. The rest of the second story contained our bedroom and a further guest bedroom.

But our favorite thing—or, at least, the funniest thing—about our house was that it came with an outhouse. And not just an outhouse, a "double-seater." I will never forget Mr. Dixon's reaction when we had invited the family over for dinner and drinks. He took one look at the two holes cut into the seating plank and said, "Jeez, you must be in love to do that!"

Even in those days, building an arena was expensive, and I was grateful to my father for lending us the money to both build it and erect fencing. We were young, hungry, and motivated which carried us along each twelve-hour day. Leaving Deerwood at seven in the morning, Birgit and I would arrive at Erdenheim in our green Mustang, which usually announced our arrival with a series of backfires, and be on our first horse by eight o'clock. Our working students would have studied the list of horses to groom and tack. Between our arrival and one in the afternoon, I worked eight of them. Then it was time for the lunch Birgit had packed for us each morning, and remaining ever faithful to my life-long habit of taking an afternoon nap to recharge, she would drive us back home while I got my shut-eye. Upon our return to Deerwood, there were five horses waiting for us in full training, and those schooling sessions began at two o'clock and were finished at six. Don't ask me how we managed it, but somehow, in between all of that, I was also teaching people who trailered in for lessons. This went on every day, six days a week.

One of those who drove in for lessons was Lynn Lendrowski—she came very steadily, for as long as Birgit and I remained in Pennsylvania. You never know where a relationship with a student might take you, and when she and her husband, a meteorologist, moved to Hawaii, she didn't have to ask twice if I'd consider flying to Hawaii to teach clinics she'd arranged. Talk about a paid vacation! Birgit and I thoroughly enjoyed each visit, and it was great to have her back on the mainland when they moved to Virginia afterward.

Another student was actually my very first client at Deerwood, Nancy Polozker. Nancy moved from Michigan to work with me. At the same time, Mary Anne McPhail, whom I'd met when I was a guest instructor at Violet Hopkins's USDF seminars, had a Swedish horse that she'd asked me to ride. I did, the horse went well, and I had a new client. The horse, Navarro, had great success, going all the way to Grand

Prix, and after Mary Anne had enjoyed her journey with him, he was sold to another student of mine, Jane Landau, who rode him in her very first Grand Prix.

Back at Erdenheim, things were rolling along uneventfully that summer. I'd even been given a beautiful space to be used as my own office, which Jerry Baker had remarked was "too nice a room to be used as an office." But my office, it became, and I was happy to have it. And as the year ebbed into autumn, I noticed both Jerry and Michael Matz packing up to head to Florida for three and half months, and an audacious idea began to form. I asked for a meeting with Mr. Dixon, and when I explained to him that it would be a good idea to also take the dressage horses south for the winter, he replied, "Why don't you fly down and take a look at it?"

The obvious contact to make was Mary Phelps, whom I'd met at horse shows with her camera around her neck, taking shots of competitors. Giving her a call, I asked if she might know of a barn that would be available to lease through the winter, and, in true Mary style, she mused over it for maybe half a day before getting back to me and saying, "There's a German couple who've immigrated to Indiantown, about 45 minutes northwest of Palm Beach. They bought a Standardbred farm. Nothing fancy, but it's a nice, big farm with fifteen stalls." Grateful for this lead, I thanked her and contacted the couple: Gisela and Howald Pferdekämper. When I called their farm, it was the barn manager who answered the phone, and I explained why I was calling. He took the message, and within half an hour, Gisela called from Germany to say she'd be back in a week's time, and in the meantime, we made arrangements to meet.

It was a treat to leave the chill of Pennsylvania behind us as we flew into West Palm Beach, rented a car, and drove to meet our potential winter landlords. It couldn't have gone better: lots of wine, lots of laughs, and the facility was just fine. The stable had been built to withstand hurricanes, and the stalls were solid cinderblock. Gisela announced she'd build us an outdoor arena, which she did—basically just dragging the ever-present sand around. It's not my intention to be at all derogatory about her effort; that's the way things were in those days, and I think it says something (what, I'm not sure) that regardless of less-than-perfectly manicured footing, our horses stayed sound!

By January 5th, Birgit and I (along with Laurie Stanton, who'd never seen the ocean, so we decided to bring her) arrived with a dozen horses total, including mounts belonging to the Dixons, the Steinkrauses, and Mary Anne McPhail, plus our own Ostergaard horses. For the second time in my life, I felt rather like a pioneer: after becoming, to the best of my knowledge, the first nationally accredited Danish *berider* to arrive in the United States, now I was also the first dressage trainer to take a string of dressage horses to Florida for the winter season.

However, there was very little going on during our first season in the "Sunshine State," and we simply enjoyed working the horses, who also seemed grateful for the respite from long northern winters. When March arrived and we were heading back, we learned that near Wildwood, Florida, just north of Orlando, were one or two shows. We decided to compete there, as did Anne Gribbons, and we found ourselves all staying at the Days Inn in Wildwood. We became so bored between the shows, with precious little to do, that, absurdly, we decided to throw a mock wedding for my cousin Hanne, who had flown over for a visit.

The entire affair was featured in an upcoming issue of *Dressage and Eventing* magazine, complete with ridiculous photos of my cousin wearing a beige nightgown, with a "tiara" made of tinfoil, made resplendent by a peacock feather sticking out the top. I may have made the cover of the magazine in my top hat and tails aboard Jubi, but for the "wedding," the top hat and tails were being worn by the "groom," our other friend from Denmark, Tommy. As he had been the one who had jokingly warned Birgit that I wouldn't take her to America, now it was his turn to experience marital bliss in the United States. At least until dinnertime. I tottered up the aisle to give away my cousin, her arm linked through mine, as I had dressed as a doddering old man, leaning heavily on a walking stick and using my German Shepherd as a guide dog. Even Anne Gribbons took part, wearing her bowler hat and acting the part of the minister to "bless" the couple. Birgit looked ravishing in a plastic clothing bag, and Ellin led "the choir" in a rendition of "Jingle Bells."

Bill and Sis Steinkraus somehow sat through the entire wedding, even bringing wedding gifts. Afterwards, there was singing and speeches that lasted far too late. By morning, our "groom" had disappeared, perhaps in search of a Bloody Mary and an aspirin.

I still have that 1981 copy of *Dressage and Eventing*, and the photos of the competitions and our "wedding" always bring a smile. It was Anne who covered the event for the magazine, as well as the shows, and what a long time ago it now seems, especially reading the last line of her article: "I have no doubt that the Florida dressage circuit will become to the world of dressage what the Sunshine Circuit is to the hunter and jumper crowd."

In our wildest dreams, none of us could have imagined just how enormous it indeed would become.

CHAPTER
24

TRAIN OF GOOD FORTUNE

A T THE END OF THAT FIRST FLORIDA SEASON, Birgit and I were growing a touch weary of sunburned ears and noses, the creeping mugginess, and the intensifying heat. We had, however, accomplished much, and I had thoroughly enjoyed witnessing the early growth of the Florida dressage circuit through our friendship with Howald and Gisela.

Howald was a consummate businessman, and had the foresight to invest in a large piece of land, as he recognized the potential for this to become a playground for wealthy American riders who wanted their homes and barns on a handful of acres, with a common competition area essentially in their backyard. He purchased something like two hundred acres, and expanded their own personal estate—they built our stable, an elegant home for themselves, and an apartment for Birgit and me.

Everything was within walking distance of our barn, quite close together, and this became White Fences. While Howald deservedly gets credit for his foresight, the part many people don't know is that it was something else to watch Gisela roll up her sleeves and go to work. I've never seen anything like it! When I say she constructed the arenas, the landscaping, and even the judging huts, I mean she was doing exactly that: moving earth herself, hammering, sawing, lugging lumber, and digging.

Afterward, when all was finished and they advertised White Fences, they used a photograph of Howald, Gisela, their two young boys, and the family German Shepherd. Best of all was the caption;

Howald had earned his doctorate in economics, which gave him the credibility to state, "Just What The Doctor Ordered." They called this new development Hannover Farms, but unfortunately, it didn't sell. Probably the best money they spent was on a publicist who told them to get rid of the Hannover name, put up some white fences, and call it White Fences. It seems ridiculous that this is all it took, and it didn't happen overnight, but with the change of name came success, and the development is, of course, still known by this name today.

At the same time, Howald and I discussed how to stir up further interest, and, drawing upon my European competition experience, I suggested we create a big horse show and give it the prestigious name of The Palm Beach Dressage Derby. For the first three or four years, it continued as it had for me in Denmark, with riders exchanging horses at the Prix St Georges and Intermediare level. I was delighted to see my friend Patrick Burssens win the inaugural event, and Danish rider Kenneth Dyrby finished right behind him.

With the season behind us and the Floridian heat cranking up in earnest, I suggested to Birgit, "Maybe we should take a little vacation after we get back to Pennsylvania, and take a trip to Vermont?" As she had never seen it, she couldn't quite visualize the love affair I had with the state, after all the clinics I had taught there. And, as ever, I was toying with the idea of perhaps buying a piece of land.

Birgit was agreeable to the idea, and off we went, in search of cool, dry air and a landscape that was far more appealing than the monotonous flat, sandy stretches of Florida. We met up with a realtor, who showed us various properties neither of us found appealing. Taking a break, Birgit and I went out to dinner in Manchester, and over a glass of wine, she murmured dejectedly that even if we hadn't found anything, it didn't really matter, because we probably couldn't afford it anyway. I, however, wasn't ready to throw in the towel.

The following day, we ventured into Chester, where we stopped by a company that built log homes and enjoyed fantasizing about such a possibility. By lunch, however, we were looking at the classified ads in the local newspaper simply for raw land. Our waitress took note, and after she took our order, asked, "Looking for anything in particular?" Normally, waitresses are tipped for good service, but on this day at the

Inn on the Green in Chester, I have to say she gave us an even bigger tip when she said, "Go two houses down and see Bud Oberg—he's the local realtor and he knows everything."

Doing as we were told, we approached Bud in his office, and were somewhat shocked when he didn't ask us anything—not our budget, nor even our names. All he needed to know was what we volunteered as our goal: a sizable piece of land, maybe a hundred acres, with a beautiful view. Bud flipped through some papers on his desk, glanced up, and said, "Okay. Give me an hour and come back."

We promptly returned one hour later, and Bud reported he had but one suitable listing—the half-mile driveway, which, of course, is what we bought. It still makes me smile to think again how Birgit, within 12 hours, went from being almost despondent to marveling over the view of what would become our next Deerwood Farm, stating matter-of-factly, "I think we should take it."

In that first year, popping back and forth on quick visits from Pennsylvania, we became friends with Henry and Janet Schurink, a lovely Dutch couple about 20 years our senior who were fellow immigrants. That gave us a connection that only other immigrants can fully understand. In fact, Henry told me several times over the years that when he first saw my only full-page ad taken out in *Dressage & Combined Training*, he said to himself, "Oh, well, here comes another one..." They became clients until Janet stopped riding in her 80s, but remained life-long friends of ours. It was a pleasure to do clinics at their Doornhof Farm in Shaftsbury, and while Henry has sadly passed away, I am delighted to report that Janet, now in her 90s, is living proof that age is just a number, as she continues feeding all the horses in her barn and isn't above doing a bit of mucking as well! In fact, she recently told me in an email that there was no reason at all I couldn't continue to teach well into my 90s! If you're reading this, Janet, I'll agree—but only if I can continue to come to your farm!

Back at the original Deerwood, in Pennsylvania, I had been inspired by George Morris, who had successfully held a hunter-jumper "unmounted clinic." It made sense to me that the same sort of thing could be done with dressage—a sort of lecture series—and this became the first dressage "symposium," a type of event that is now commonplace. What would make ours unique was that I would encourage a dialogue with attendees, both soliciting questions from them and asking for their responses. For example, I would have a horse ridden in shoulder-in, and then ask the audience their opinion: Had it been correct? If not, why? What could be done to improve it?

I approached Mr. Dixon to ask if it would be possible to hold such an event at Erdenheim. Ever generous, he agreed, and as the date drew near, we were delighted to have such a successful turnout for our inaugural event. That very first unmounted clinic resulted in 160 auditors, who began arriving Friday afternoon to simply observe us training our horses. Saturday's program began with us backing horses, with three horses in each level from Training through Grand Prix. We did basic work with them all, then demonstrated foundational movements on the first day and more advanced movements on the following day. And during it all, a running dialogue continued between me and the auditors. It was amazing to us that people had traveled from fifteen different states to attend, and we knew we were onto something pretty special. During the evening, Birgit and I hosted a party for all attendees in the common area at Erdenheim: a huge room with a kitchen. I remember losing my voice that night, as well as on Sunday afternoon.

The unmounted clinic became an annual affair that went on for five years at Erdenheim (and, years later, continued at our farm in Vermont, as well as Potomac Horse Center), and I remain grateful for the help we received from Amanda Maxwell, who was a hunter-jumper trainer interested in dressage. I had taught well-run clinics to her students at her barn, and could tell right away she was sharp, detail-oriented, and professional—the perfect person to ask to organize my events. She and her husband, Timothy, became good friends of mine.

Those unmounted clinics were always held during the first or second week in December. Finishing up one Sunday, I turned to the auditors and asked, "Anyone have any questions?"

Ellin called out, "You can't quit yet, there's a surprise coming!" Like a small budget knock-off of White Christmas, without Bing Crosby or Danny Kaye, the back door of the indoor arena was opened and in came "Santa," who was, in reality, our barn employee Howard, who had been persuaded to wear the getup and pull a wagon that held Ellin and four working students. They sang a highly original and very funny parody of "The 12 Days of Christmas," in which they changed all the verses to be about Birgit and me. It was the perfect end to the clinic, and a heartwarming and sweet gesture that I've always treasured.

Some people have certain periods of time in their lives that they remember as all of a piece, whether fondly or with horror. It might be a particular day, week, month, year, or even multiple years, when everything seemed to go well or completely wrong.

For me, I would have to say that from the moment I arrived in America all the way through the late 1980s, it felt as if I were on an unstoppable train of good fortune. I had—we had—worked hard each and every day, but we all know other riders and trainers that are just as dedicated yet don't quite catch the lucky breaks; for those lucky breaks I did catch, I remain grateful.

Looking back, it's as if each memory flips over like a page on a calendar, one after the other, year by year.

In the early '80s, Max Gahwyler asked whether I'd be interested in working with students at the prestigious Ox Ridge, an hour north of New York City, teaching clinics each month. I was given the title of "Director of Dressage at Ox Ridge Hunt Club," which sounded very impressive indeed.

Around this same time, Jimmy Wofford was sent by the USET to be a guinea pig of sorts and take a lesson with me, and his positive feedback led the USET to open the door to working with American 3-Day-Event Team riders, improving their dressage, in the lead-up to the 1984 Los Angeles Olympic Games where they took gold. What a privilege it was to work with those riders. I remember being asked by the Team, following one of those clinics, to write a critique of each rider. For Bruce Davidson, I wrote, "I'd take him on as a dressage rider anytime." And for J. Michael Plumb, whose home must be filled to the brim with medals and trophies despite his less-than-exemplary position, I wrote, "Mike Plumb—who am I to tell him to sit up straight?"

The chance to work with yet more talented event riders came via the Canadian 3-Day Team, which was being coached by David O'Connor. While David obviously focused on the cross-country and show jumping,

I worked intensely on improving their dressage scores, and it was great to see the Team win silver at the World Games in Kentucky.

At the same time, I was also coaching Becky Holder, an alternate rider on the US Team aboard her horse Courageous Comet. I met Becky during clinics I was teaching in Minnesota, and about six months before the World Games, she asked if I would work privately with her, including warming her up before she went down the centerline on the big day. It was a thrill for us both, as she nailed her test and received the best American score in dressage, finishing 5th out of 80 horses. Nearly as much fun was the glowing press we both received following her triumph.

My passion for real estate was given free rein to explore, and in 1985, Birgit and I bought our first condo on Singer Island, a narrow barrier island just north of Palm Beach, with beautiful, pristine beaches. We couldn't afford one of the top floors with breathtaking views far out across the Atlantic, but our third-floor residence did give us a lovely dual aspect: ocean on one side, and the Intercoastal Waterway on the other. It was a bit of a drive to get to White Fences during those winter seasons, but knowing that we had a place of our own gave us a sense of home away from home.

As Birgit and I were frequently flying back and forth to Denmark on horse-scouting trips, we thought it would be useful to invest in a summer home about 45 minutes north of Copenhagen—right on the sound between Denmark and Sweden, called Hornbaek. We only used it part-time, while horse shopping and on vacations, so it remained available for our families to use the rest of the time.

Those horse-buying trips abroad were always an adventure, and in the days before cell phones and movie screens onboard, it was customary, even pleasant, to chat with whomever might be seated next to you as you both made your way across the Atlantic. During one such flight, on the way home to the States, it just so happened that I was booked on the same flight as the young horse, Anjin, that Birgit had purchased in Denmark. In those days, it was common for both people and cargo—in this case, horses—to fly together, although the human passengers were seldom aware of the hooved passengers behind them. But there Anjin was, stabled behind the last "wall" in the plane, and I had even been allowed to go back and visit her before the flight was boarded—how easy were the days of travel before 9/11!

As the plane took off and climbed to its cruising altitude, I struck up a friendly chat with the Swedish businessman in the seat next to me. As one does, I asked about his trip, and he explained he was obliged by his business to travel. He then, in his turn, asked me about my business. I replied that I was a trainer, and told him I had a horse behind us, in the back of the plane. Evidently he thought I was mentally impaired and off my meds; it was as if a door snapped shut between us. I couldn't get another word out of him, nor would he even look at me. I was completely dismissed!

Meanwhile, back in the States, my longtime friend Raul de Leon, working alongside gold medalist Tad Coffin, had been hired by Westmoreland Davis Institute in Virginia. The idea was that both Raul and Tad would be on the faculty to both oversee and instruct the potential professional trainers who came to live and study at the Institute for half a year. These students were lucky to take part in lessons with the likes of Raul and Tad Coffin several days a week, and I was happy to oblige when asked to teach clinics as well. The fly in the ointment was that these were "group lessons," and any trainer will nod in agreement over how taxing teaching groups of riders can be. It was extremely important to me to be completely professional and give each rider as much personal attention as possible, but the Institute kept cramming more and more students into these groups, until each lesson was bursting at the seams. I gave it my all, and do not exaggerate when I say that out of the thousands of clinics I've taught in my life, those were the most exhausting. I would leave and barely manage the drive home, I was so drained.

A bit easier was my appointment to the Institute's Advisory Committee, with each member officially representing one discipline. It was quite a feather in my cap to be representing dressage while U.S. Team coaches Jack LeGoff and Bert de Némethy oversaw the eventing and the show jumping respectively.

I continued to teach as many clinics as I could add to my schedule, and it's been a wonderful thing to maintain many of those relationships, as well as to hear that I have helped influence those who went on to become successful professionals. Bill Warren was one. I met Bill originally through the clinics that Janet Black—a South African who was already well known in New England as a teacher and judge—organized in Rhode Island. Bill was working diligently to get his judging credentials, and needed to compete at Grand Prix to earn his "S" license to be able to judge at the FEI levels. Nowadays, Bill is on his way to earning the prestigious Level 4 license.

Not all clinics were filled with such noteworthy riders, of course. Some were simply...baffling. For years, my friend Fran Horn put together countless clinics for me on Long Island at the rather smart-sounding Gold Coast Equestrian Center. Anyone who has ever participated in a clinic knows that tardiness is not tolerated, and riders are expected not only to be as neat and tidy as their well-groomed horses, but punctual to the minute.

At this particular clinic, the slot for the 10:15 lesson rolled around and there was no student to be seen. At 10:20, a big Mercedes pulled up and out stepped a mother and her roly-poly son, who then mounted his equally roly-poly pony, held by the child's groom, tacked and waiting. At this point, there were only 30 minutes remaining for his lesson, and it was clear the child had no idea how to ride. Pulling my cap down a little further on my brow, I cringed at the thought that one of my high-level European colleagues might walk in to see how I was faring as a U.S. trainer!

Doing what I could, I worked on the child's position, while he made it evident by his sullen expression that he wasn't the least bit interested in having a lesson. The pony carried him safely as he alternately slumped and bounced around in the saddle at walk and trot. I managed to teach them both a few steps of leg-yield, and was more than a little relieved when the next student appeared on deck a few minutes later. Later in the afternoon, Fran, who always enjoys a good joke, made a point of walking into the arena to interrupt my lesson and relay a message loudly for all to hear: that the kid's mother "just called to say his testicles are killing him and what should she do?"

I thought for a moment. "Tell her to get him breeches instead of tight jeans."

On the other end of the spectrum were some of the nicest and most enjoyable people I've ever met: Fred and Peggy Furth. The Furths lived a couple of hours north of San Francisco, in Healdsburg, and happened to employ a former groom and rider from Erdenheim, John (who was returning to his native California), who used to work for Jerry Baker.

Out of the blue, I got a call from John one day, telling me, "I have this very serious client I work for and they're going to be flying their private jet to Philly to look for a Grand Prix horse. They're very serious about buying, but the horse has to be tall." The only appropriate horse we had at the time was a gelding called Hadrian that Birgit had bought as a three-year-old in '79, but I was feeling somewhat reluctant, as the horse had just made it to top level. Discussing it back and forth, Birgit and I decided that we'd only sell Hadrian for a specific amount, but if the Furths met that price, we'd let him go. Upon meeting Fred and Peggy, it was clear why their potential mount had to be tall, as Peggy was quite tall herself! She tried Hadrian and bought him; this was to be only the first horse sale I did with them, which led to many more to come.

Fred was colorful, had a great sense of humor, and had been featured on the cover of *Time* magazine as one of the "One Hundred Most Successful Attorneys in America." Both of them were a joy to be around—not to mention, they spoiled us rotten. Birgit and I were flown twice to Europe on their private jet, hopping from country to country like jet-setters, and housed in such hotels as the Four Seasons in Hamburg and the Dorchester in London. Everything was first-class, and traveling with them was like going on holiday.

Indulging in another passion, the Furths opened Chalk Hill Winery, and it was always a pleasure to fly out to teach clinics in that beautiful part of the country. They even flew horses from California to Florida to continue to work with me while I was there for the winter season. Of all the places and grand adventures we had, one particularly happy memory is being flown across the country to ride Hadrian, after they had bought him, in front of a packed grandstand at a combination wine-tasting and dressage exhibition at a local fairground. The local papers gave it the headline, "Dressage in the Wine Country," and it was a spectacular event.

It wasn't long before "the third person in our marriage"— real estate—inspired me to look for an apartment in Manhattan. I had always loved New York City, and would look for any excuse to spend time there.

However, I also knew how expensive it was, and so I figured if we could rent it out, at least it would pay for itself. It still boggles my mind that we were able to snap up an eighth-floor condo, complete with doorman, on 32nd Street, between Lexington and 3rd Avenues, which was a four-minute walk to the Empire State Building.

I had this thing—as ridiculous as it may sound—where whenever I bought a new piece of real estate, I was determined to spend a night there before it was rented out. And determined I must have been, because it was November, freezing, and I had to park a block away. Birgit, sensible and deciding to remain warm, said, "Be my guest," as I told her I was going to be loaded down like a pack mule, carrying a folding Army cot, folding chair, and stand just to sleep in my latest residence overnight.

The following morning, I had to be out of there by seven in the morning as I had to teach a clinic on Long Island, and after dressing, refolding all my "furniture," and gathering the blankets, topped with my pillow, I realized I would have to carry the load to where my car was parked. I prayed I'd be the only person on the elevator, as I must have looked crazy. Pushing the "down" button, I breathed easy as the elevator descended, uninterrupted, several floors until—dammit—it slowed and stopped on the second floor. In walked an elderly lady, who took one look at me and my heavy load, blinked, and asked, "Are you going on a picnic?"

I couldn't stop laughing, and explained as best I could in my broken English that I had just wanted to stay there for the night. Whether or not this made any sense to her, I'll never know. She was good enough to smile at my dilemma.

The 1980s had been an incredible decade for Birgit and me, and we began talking earnestly about selling our Pennsylvania farm in the next couple of years and moving to our property in Vermont. To even consider such an idea meant I was confident enough to no longer feel that I needed to be centrally located. But it did mean I needed to speak with the Dixons.

After a decade at Erdenheim, I knew Ellin had ambitions to become a trainer in her own right, as well as to compete internationally. I encouraged her to return to Germany with Gibraltar, her world-class horse, to work with George Theodorescu. And so one February day at their beautiful Florida farm, I resigned from my position with the Dixons. In the dressage world, to maintain a close, friendly student-trainer relationship for ten years was as rare then as it is today.

Ellin and I decided to throw a "Going Our Separate Ways" party, which took place around the large pool at the Dixons' Wellington farm. Quite a few of my other students and all of the Erdenheim working students were in attendance, and in the end, somehow Ellin and I ended up fully clothed in the pool, embracing in a hug.

I feel a deep, personal satisfaction that Ellin and her husband, Bruce Miller, experienced joy and great success aboard two horses that I trained while at Erdenheim: Windsor (whom Ellin rode on the Pan Am team that same year as my resignation), and Atlantis (whom Bruce took to multiple FEI wins and championships for years to come). We had had a terrific run together, and now it was time to work toward taking up residence at the farm which would become Birgit's and my home for the next 39 years.

CHAPTER
25

THE BIGGEST MISTAKE OF MY LIFE

I N DRESSAGE, THE TERM "FORWARD!" is often used to improve nearly every aspect of training, and in our own lives, Birgit and I were thinking "forward!" as well, focusing on a future with new horses, a new farm, and new adventures.

And then what can only be described as a gut punch came out of the blue. As with all calamities, a bit of backstory is needed, beginning with a bitter piece of irony.

When I leased Long Valley from Mr. Trillich, he suggested that it would be a good idea for me to carry insurance. Certainly, when I lived in Europe, I had heard that America was a litigious country, and people would sue each other at the drop of a hat.

"For example," Mr Trillich explained, "say you're teaching a dentist, and he falls off the horse and gets hurt. Not only could you be liable for his injury, but potentially millions more, should his injury prevent him from continuing to work."

It was good advice, yet I didn't follow it. This was the biggest mistake of my life.

I just never believed I'd actually get sued by a dentist.

A lawsuit that would occupy our thoughts for thirteen months, filling us alternately with disbelief and dread, was the farthest thing from our minds when Birgit and I bought our first horse together after our marriage, in 1979.

Elbiskus was a yearling colt by the Trakehner stallion Ibikus. Elbiskus was approved as a stallion in 1981, and we shipped him over as a three-year-old, when he became approved in the States as well. We would take Elbiskus with us to Florida during the winter seasons, and he would return to breeding duties from March to June until 1984. By age nine, he was confirmed at Grand Prix and became Birgit's very first Grand Prix horse. As with all our horses, if someone offers us a specific price, we will sell, and so it was with Elbiskus, whom we sold in 1990.

Luckily for us, Ellen had bred her Swedish mares to Elbiskus, and in 1983 we bought two foals he had sired. Ellen kept alive her personal tradition of naming her horses exclusively after fine wines (I never knew her to name a horse "Budweiser" or "Coors Light"), and these two foals were named after champagne: one was called Clicquot, and the other was the subject of the rest of this story; I'll call him "K."

Trying to decide which one of us would take which foal, Birgit and I struck up a deal: because K appeared to be the taller and more substantial of the two, he would become mine, and Birgit would take on the more refined Clicquot. It made sense to leave both foals with Ellen until they turned three, at which point we would then back and produce each one independently, doing what we chose with each.

At this time, I was still serving as director of dressage at Ox Ridge, and one particular student came faithfully to all my clinics on an older horse that had developed soundness issues. After one clinic, she said to me, "If you come across a younger horse, I will be in the market," and my thoughts fell upon K. He was presently being backed and proving to be not only a nice prospect, but sensible and level-headed. Not once had he offered a buck or any type of naughtiness.

One weekend during late summer, this student and her husband came to Quakertown to watch Birgit and Marija Trishman, our Swedish working student, continue K's early training. Marija was in the saddle while Birgit coached from the ground, and it was evident to both the student and her husband that, while K was obviously green, he was comfortably walking, trotting, and cantering under saddle with no issues. They liked what they saw, had him vetted, and bought him without a hitch. K went to be boarded at an upscale facility north of New York City, and it was always nice to receive the occasional phone call from his new owner as she gave us enthusiastic reports about how well he was doing and how happy she was with him.

It's always satisfying when a client is happy and remains a friend. Because of this, and because we always enjoyed going to New York, Birgit and I decided to choose her husband as our regular dentist, traveling regularly to his practice in the city for the next couple of years.

Bad news travels fast in the horse world; two years later, the terrible news came to us third-hand that, during a lesson with this student's regular instructor (well-known and respected), K had picked up a counter-canter, lost his balance, and hit the wall, killing the student. Birgit and I were horrified, and without delay, I telephoned her husband to send our deepest condolences, which he seemingly appreciated.

About three months later, a dental reminder card arrived in the mail, which was reassuring to receive. While my former student's husband wasn't a horseman by any means, the card, to me, seemed to symbolize that everything would continue as usual, and I promptly scheduled an appointment to have my teeth cleaned. It would be good to see him, I thought, and see how he was doing.

I arrived a little before my noon appointment a couple of weeks later, and walked up to the front desk to check in, finding myself second in line behind a tall man in a dark suit. I just had the time to think, "Good, only one person ahead of me," when the man in the suit swiveled around and pointedly asked, "Are you Gunnar Ostergaard?" I replied that I was, and he handed me a stack of papers, declaring, "You have four weeks to respond to this lawsuit," before turning to the door and departing.

I had been set up.

In a flash, I understood how serious this was, and asked the receptionist if I could speak with my now former dentist; she replied that he was with a patient. Sitting down, I took a couple of deep breaths, put the papers under my arm, and then left.

I had planned to combine two appointments that day, the second being with a doctor for an ear infection. Walking toward that office, stunned, I was nearing Lexington and 32nd—close to my apartment. Knowing there was a bar a couple of blocks away, I made a beeline for it. If ever anyone needed a drink, I did, but I chose to order a cup of coffee instead as I pored over the stack of papers I'd spread out over the small, round tabletop. In complete disbelief, I read that I was being sued for $20 million "for having sold a dangerous horse and trained it recklessly."

$20 million? K? The well-mannered, well-started youngster I had sold them two years ago, who had been the subject of enthusiastic phone calls ever since—not to mention he'd been moved to a different state under different instruction? *Are you kidding me?* I thought, but I couldn't stop my heart from hammering in my chest. I paid my check and returned to the streets of Manhattan, oblivious to the steady drone of traffic and construction surrounding me, and called Birgit from a payphone, having to speak loudly to be heard over the din.

When I returned home, Birgit shared my incredulity, and we both found comfort by remarking to each other that the lawsuit was absurd and there was no way we could be held responsible. Having never been sued before, the very presence of the paperwork still weighed heavily on us, and the only person I could think to contact was the husband of Amanda Maxwell, who had organized so many clinics for me. Timothy was a young up-and-coming attorney within a prestigious firm. It's almost comical now, thinking back to how startled I was when he requested that we courier the paperwork to him at once, straight to his Philadelphia office, which would cost us $25. That seemed like a lot of money to spend—I had no idea of the fortune I would be spending to defend us over the next thirteen months.

After Timothy received the paperwork, the voicemail he left for us was nothing short of ominous. "This is very, very serious," he said. "If you're at home Saturday afternoon, I'd like to come over and explain this."

It goes without saying that that Saturday afternoon was the worst Saturday afternoon of our lives. It was cold; we had a fire going. Birgit and I sat on the sofa, shocked, as we were told firmly that this lawsuit could ruin us—despite the fact that we had had nothing to do with the accident.

We had hoped Timothy would be more positive, but despite his kind, professional manner, everything he had to say was the opposite of what we had longed to hear. It didn't matter that we had backed and sold a safe, quality youngster. It didn't matter that the horse had been moved to another state, under another trainer. And, preposterously, it didn't matter that the accident had happened a full two years after we sold him.

"This is America," Timothy replied to our queries of disbelief. "And anyone can sue anyone."

Of course, I had heard this while living in Denmark. Still, I'd been raised in a country where if one person sues another and loses, the loser is obliged to pay all court costs for both parties, and so lawsuits were relatively rare. Somehow, I hadn't really believed the litigious reputation of America.

Now I did. My eyes swept over the small living room of this farm we had worked so hard to make our own.

"What would happen if we said we had no money?" I asked hopefully.

"It's not that easy," Timothy answered. "Listen, these guys will trace every stream of revenue you have, and it's very easy for them to check and trace your accounts and find out what properties you own."

I immediately thought of our newly acquired land in Vermont, and the Manhattan and Florida condos.

"They can take those?" I asked, glancing at Birgit.

"They can take everything," he said. "They can also garnish your wages for life."

This was an almighty blow.

Timothy went on to tell us what to expect in the coming days and weeks. He used terms like "the long arm of the law," and talked about the necessity of our writing an "affidavit." Birgit and I would later find some comic relief in these things as, in our broken English, we struggled to grasp their meanings, but one thing was clear: the costs of defending ourselves would be astronomical.

Because we were being sued in New York, Timothy said we would require a meeting with one of the senior partners in his New York office, Mr. Linsemeyer. We agreed and arranged a late afternoon meeting for five o'clock.

Coming at the end of a full day of riding and teaching, Birgit and I made the hour-and-a-half drive to Park Avenue that raw November afternoon, while Timothy took the train. We parked our car, met downstairs in the lobby, and I remember it took ages for the elevator to climb, floor by floor, all the way up: 38, 39, 40.... Finally we stepped out and were introduced to Mr. Linsemeyer, a distinguished, slender gentleman in his early 60s who ushered us into his office. It was a cavernous room with a bank of windows that gave us an expansive view of Manhattan, now lit up as the sun had set. I stood there, utterly overwhelmed, and thought to myself, "We're going to be helping him pay for this office." It also occurred to me that our own condo was a five-minute walk away from this office—maybe we should have held off buying it!

As pleasant as Mr Linsemeyer was, he wasn't impressed by Birgit's and my explanation that the lawsuit was ridiculous and unrealistic. He explained that we had to respond. Thinking that presenting myself as a professional would be helpful, I even produced a couple of magazines in which I was featured on the cover. This, he felt, was positive, but we received the same story Timothy had conveyed: we could face financial ruin, and might lose everything. Noting our crestfallen expressions, he was kind enough to stress that the firm would do its best to keep the cost as low as possible. We shook hands, thanked him, and entered the elevator once again; the steel box felt as a metaphor for our collective mood as it descended lower and lower.

Once in the lobby, we thanked Timothy and said our goodbyes as he left for the train station to return to Philadelphia. Birgit and I walked silently in the dark toward the parking deck, huddling in our coats against a stiff, wintry wind. Our day from hell wasn't done with us yet: upon finding our car, we also found we had a flat tire. I'm not the least bit mechanical, and to be honest, I wasn't even sure where the jack and tire iron were kept in our car. It took ages to find someone who could help us, and finally, when we pulled out of the parking garage and turned the car toward the ninety-minute drive home, we alternated between complete silence and trying to lift each other up, confidently stating that we could win—there was no way we could be held responsible. Neither of us spoke the thought that remained looming at the front of our brains: that we could also lose.

What followed, for days and weeks, was disconcerting: nothing. There were no meetings, just periodic phone calls from Timothy. And then the bills began to arrive. Holding my breath, I opened the first envelope from the firm. My hand wasn't shaking, but my stomach was, when my eyes took in the invoice total of $6,000—and this was just the beginning!

There was no time to waste, and I count myself fortunate in that I have always had more than enough work offered to me whenever I wanted it. The clinics I taught generally had waiting lists, and it was time to take advantage of every opportunity. News of the lawsuit had circulated around the dressage world, and we received heartfelt support and sympathy. Yet sympathy had nothing to do with the work I now scheduled—I telephoned each and every clinic organizer who had been pressing to get another date from me, and I might just have set the world record for the number of clinics taught all over the country to raise the cash.

In the meantime, with this ominous cloud over our heads, Birgit and I could only move forward as we knew how to do. The Florida season arrived, and we headed down as usual, and kept training, competing, and teaching. Timothy checked in with the hopeful news that the New York attorneys were working on moving the case to Pennsylvania because I had been "lured" to New York with that dental reminder. If they were successful in this venture, the costs for the plaintiff would be much higher. Just that, alone, might be enough for him to drop the suit.

We had taken Marija along with us to Florida, and when she wasn't working for us, she ran a small business on the side—riding a few horses that belonged to other people—for some extra money. We had always thoroughly enjoyed having Marija on our team. She was perpetually good-natured, no matter how hard the work or how late at night we might need to phone her. She worked quickly and diligently—so much so that when we took on another girl to ease Marija's burden, the girl, who was hopelessly slow and disorganized, came to see us a few days later, forlornly stating, "Marija says she's going to kill me." It was all I could do not to laugh, and I think I said something to the effect that I would have a word with Marija and sort things out.

A few days later, I was standing in the arena, explaining something to a student who had halted her horse to listen. As she glanced up, her eyes widened, and she said, "I think your girl, Marija, just had a fall and it looks like she's not getting up."

Marija had not been wearing a helmet, and we ran over and found her unconscious. An ambulance was called immediately, and once admitted to the hospital, she remained in a coma for several days. Her brain injury was traumatic, and with palpable relief we rejoiced when she regained consciousness. However, it wasn't an overnight recovery—Marija didn't recognize her husband, whom she'd just married! She spent nearly a month in the hospital before she was released, rehabbing with focused dedication and slowly improving.

Before long, the Florida season concluded and we headed back north, the lawsuit still looming over us. And then we had a bit of luck: we heard through the grapevine that our plaintiff had sold K for the same amount of money we'd sold him for. This was a huge tactical error: how could he possibly explain why he decided to sell such a "dangerous" horse for a substantial amount of money? Had K truly been such a menace, surely the plaintiff would have put him down, or given him away to someone fully informed.

It took very little detective work on Birgit's and my part to find K's new owner, a woman named Suzy who lived in New Hampshire. I had given her trainer a lesson somewhere in the northeast, and, remembering his name, made a quick call in which we learned that indeed, he was now training K. We arranged a meeting with the four of us at a restaurant in Keene, New Hampshire. The information they gave us benefited our case greatly: K had been shown at Devon, and had finished in the top five in the Young Horse Dressage Suitability Class, out of thirty entrants.

I looked directly at Suzy. "Did you ever ride K?"

She replied, "Only bareback."

Game, set, match, I thought.

It is often said, "the trend is your friend," and in this case, it felt as if the tide was turning, because while the plaintiff's attorneys moved their client's address from White Plains to Brooklyn (as this lawsuit would potentially result in a jury trial, they clearly did not want a jury of country club peers), Mr. Linsmeyer succeeded in getting the lawsuit moved from New York to Pennsylvania. We held our breath, thinking the financial obligations would lead to the plaintiff dropping the case. He didn't. This was a setback, but Birgit and I were positive we had the wind at our backs.

With the lawsuit now taking place in Pennsylvania, I retained another senior attorney from Timothy's firm, a third-generation Danish immigrant named Mr. Damsgaard. It felt good to be connected through our roots, and he was working hard to put cracks in the case. In the meantime, I was working non-stop to pay the bills that would arrive at the end of each month, in the familiar white envelope with the name of the firm printed on the top left. Month by month, I had to steel myself to read each invoice: $8,000...$10,000...$12,000!

The time drew close for the deposition in which Birgit and I, as well as Marija, would be intensely questioned. This deposition was to be videotaped and used in the trial, so everything hinged on these testimonies. There was one glaring concern: Marija. It had been only months since she'd woken up in the hospital, unable to recognize her husband. Would she remember backing K and the truth of our experiences?

It goes without saying that we were nervous as hell, as the day arrived. We parked downtown in Philadelphia and walked, hearts thumping in our chests, to the firm's office building. Everything felt intimidating: the size of the conference room, the number of attorneys present, the width of the table separating our side from theirs. Birgit and I were asked countless questions—but they were easy to answer, because all we had to do was tell the truth. And then it was Marija's turn. We held our collective breath. One slip-up, one fuzzy memory or moment of uncertainty would doom us. They began their rapid-fire exchange:

"Was K dangerous, Marija?"

"No."

"Did he ever buck you off?"

"No."

Through the entire barrage of questions, Marija was perfect. She remained calm under fire, giving detailed yet succinct replies about K's behavior: How was he to handle? What was your impression of him the very first time you rode him? How did he behave when the plaintiff's wife came to try him?

We didn't know it at the time, but that deposition would be the end of it. The case was dropped then and there, and never went to trial. It was a few days later, on a weekday morning, when Tim telephoned and relayed the wonderful news. "It's over," he said. "You can come into the Philly office to sign a lot of papers, but we'll do it during our lunch break so you won't be charged." It's a funny thing when the news you have been waiting for, hoping for, desperate for, finally arrives. Hearing there was no case didn't result in exaltation from me. There were no leaps of joy around the kitchen or punching the air in triumph. Instead, there was a slow exhalation of breath, with the knowledge that the truth we had been sure of all along had finally been confirmed.

It was a bit of a walk from the house to the arena where Birgit was riding. My bike was leaning against the courtyard stone wall, near a hefty pile of firewood I had chopped with ferocity on my darkest days. As I swung my leg over and began to pedal toward my wife, I began to think how good it would be to call our parents and give them the news. My mind raced back to that awful day when I had had to break it to them that we were being sued. It had been during our Florida season, when they'd flown over for a holiday. I'd decided to tell my father first—I'd taken him to a bar and told him the whole story, and his face had drained when he'd learned the insane amount of money the plaintiff was seeking. It had been a number my parents couldn't fathom, and they had been desperately worried. That had been the hardest thing for Birgit and me—knowing the potential impact on our families.

I could see the arena just ahead, and pedaled faster. My mind flickered to the dressage community, which had been so supportive—especially Jessica Ransehousen, who, while being interviewed for a magazine in which the lawsuit had been brought up, replied, "This would only happen to our best." Now everyone would learn we were in the clear.

I parked the bike by the arena and walked in, holding up a hand to ask Birgit to stop.

"It's over," I said, placing my hand on her knee. "The suit's been dropped."

Her reaction mirrored mine. She nodded and gave an enormous sigh of relief.

"Now we can start living again."

We didn't run out to buy champagne and toast our victory. To be honest, we didn't feel particularly victorious; this ridiculous thirteen-month ordeal had cost us $92,000. Even more galling was the fact that when we returned to Timothy's office to sign a tall stack of paperwork, one of the agreements we had to sign was that we would not countersue. That seemed completely unfair. But there was also a sense of pride I had, as we returned home, in the fact that I had managed to pay every penny by rolling up my shirtsleeves and putting my nose to the grindstone, without selling a single piece of real estate.

It was still early enough to call our parents in Denmark, and once Birgit had finished riding, she came into the house. We telephoned both sets of parents and gave them the happy update. I could just see mine huddled together on the other line, across the ocean, sharing the receiver, as I heard my mother breathe, "*Gud ske tak og lov!*" ("Praise the Lord!")

CHAPTER
26

THE BEST KIND OF CURVE BALL

I T MIGHT SOUND LIKE MADNESS, but after thirteen months of a living hell, trying to defend ourselves, I felt as if Birgit and I deserved a change of scenery, a sort of six-month holiday. At our summer home. In Denmark. With a string of horses.

We were writing a new chapter in our lives. Now in our forties, we remained energized and enthusiastic about our future, and the stars seemed to align for us. Having decided to move to Vermont, we had put our original "Deerwood" in Pennsylvania up for sale a couple of years back, and with the improvements we had made, as well as a flourishing property market, we saw an excellent return. Add to this the breathtaking generosity of Valerie Kahn, a transplant from England who had become a client and good friend—upon learning that our newest "Deerwood" in Vermont had no equestrian facilities, she offered to add several stalls to her beautiful stable for our use. Just like that. We were awestruck—who wouldn't be?

With this sort of security, both within our bank account and in having a wonderful place to train when we returned, the prospect of traveling to Denmark looked nothing but rosy. Obviously, it was to be a working holiday, but the thought of staying in our Hornbaek house, seeing all our family and friends, was exciting. We would keep working hard, training our horses and competing as well. Was there also a small part of me that wanted to return to Denmark as an American success story? I would be lying if I said no, especially as we were taking along some lovely, quality horses. I especially looked forward to seeing my old friend and mentor Gunnar Andersen. I wanted him to see firsthand that all those freezing Wednesday sessions he had devoted to me had not been in vain. Suffice it to say, I hoped he'd be proud of the trainer I had become.

We had originally planned to take just our two horses—the first being Waicon, whom Birgit had done a solid job of training up the levels, winning some good Prix St Georges tests. He was currently between levels, and while he wasn't a flashy mover, he'd proved to have a heart of gold and was bound for Grand Prix. He was later sold to Peggy Furth as a confirmed Grand Prix horse, but at this point, we were bringing him with us to train. Our second horse was a six-year-old Dutch gelding who had come to us with a silly name, and as he was proving to be a superb young prospect, we wanted to rename him. Funnily enough, we were on our way to a horse show in Massachusetts, and I suppose it was an election year, because we kept seeing signs that said "ROMNEY." We had no idea who ROMNEY was, but we liked the name, and changed the gelding's then and there. Who knew that in the years to come, Mitt and Ann Romney would become serious dressage enthusiasts and sponsors?

Birgit and I were happily anticipating our trip and spent the last month or so during the Florida season preparing for the move. The logistics we left up to Tim Dutta, who had always done international horse travel for us (except for the terrifying wedding trip!), and had everything under control. We would also be taking two young Danish people: Tilde, who had been with us in Florida and wanted to stay on to help us in Denmark; and Birgit's 17-year-old nephew, Bjarne, who had spent time with us in the States. He'd fallen in love with America and never wanted to leave. (He currently lives in San Francisco with his wife and children).

The only damper on the proceedings was that we had just lost our first beloved German Shepherd; we consoled ourselves with a plan to get a puppy in Denmark as soon as we found the right one. Our car would be shipped from Jacksonville, Florida, to the Port of Copenhagen, and we were set to go. And then fate threw us a curveball, but the very best kind of curveball.

Priscilla Endicott, the founder of the New England Dressage Association (NEDA) and then its president for something like 20 years, had been training in Germany with Walter Christensen until he died. She just happened to be a friend of Valerie Kahn. Priscilla came one day to visit Valerie, saw me ride, and not only did she ask me to take her on as a student, but also to find her a dressage prospect. That prospect appeared a month or two later, while I was in Germany. Tanzkoening was a spectacular six-year-old, and Priscilla flew over to try him and snapped him up. Now coming up on seven, he was confirmed at 4th Level and schooling the Prix St Georges. Priscilla, knowing we were leaving for six months, asked if we'd take Tanz to continue to train and compete. She didn't have to ask twice—we were delighted to include him—and when Debbie Hamilton approached me after a show and said, "Gunnar, I need to change trainers," I told her I'd be happy to take her on, but that Birgit and I were soon leaving for Denmark.

"Give me a little time to think about this," she said, and turned away. It was perhaps ten minutes later that she returned and said, "I'd like to send my horses with you."

So there we were, two months before departing for Denmark, and out of the blue we had Priscilla's Tanzkoening and Debbie's two horses: the elegant black Hanoverian Wonderful, who was currently confirmed at the small tour level, and her other Hanoverian, the dark chestnut Wandi, who, on a good day, could perform all the Grand Prix moves. I may have held my head a little higher as we arrived in Denmark with this string.

It was quite easy, even fun, to move into our summer home in Hornbaek, knowing we were going to be there for the next six months. My father kindly lent us a car temporarily so that Birgit and I could be more independent. Our own car arrived punctually, and there were more than a few surprised looks at its Florida plates as I drove into Copenhagen, but this was not to be a summer of idleness. As a matter of fact, I even returned to the States during the month of July, when everything shuts down in Denmark, to teach clinics for three weeks and maintain my client base. And fate wasn't done with us yet—right after we arrived, we bought a nice young horse in Denmark, placed a "for sale" ad in *The Chronicle*, and in the blink of an eye, a lovely couple from Florida flew over and bought him on the spot—we couldn't have started our visit on a better note.

Our horses were stabled at Barthahus, that great facility about 40 minutes north of Copenhagen, with its big indoor arena and plenty of outdoor rings. The memories of the many shows that had been held there came flooding back—between the two of us, we had won several classes there in both dressage and show jumping. This was also the facility where Gunnar Andersen had worked toward the end of his career, and where I had driven each Wednesday to receive my instruction.

And such a pleasure it was to see Grethe Knud Larsen, who had her horse boarded there. Grethe had been a student of my mentor's, and it was on her Grand Prix horse Atmospherics that Gunnar let me ride all the Grand Prix movements each week during my six years in Denmark before emigrating. She was married to the long-time president of the Danish Riding Association, Knud Larsen, and both of them had always been tremendously kind to me during my time in Denmark; I had been touched, years ago, when Knud wrote a very nice letter of recommendation upon my immigration to America.

It really felt like "Old Home Week" to school together each morning in the indoor arena for that half-year. Grethe had also been a long-time fan of Birgit's, and her adult children had competed along with Birgit in high-level jumping classes.

Birgit and I returned to so much history, and we felt warmly welcomed. We were even given our own private section in the barn, with six stalls—five for our horses, and one for our feed and hay. Things were going so swimmingly that, even though we hadn't discussed such a thing, I will admit that the thought of moving back to Denmark long-term might have flitted briefly through my mind. I suppose there is always a pull back toward one's "mother country," with the culture, traditions, and people that make up one's DNA, but within weeks, I felt a reminder of that old "law of Jante" rearing its head.

I was getting to know Debbie Hamilton's two good horses, and when she was the first owner to arrive, not long after we had gotten started, I felt I could already show her some good work. We enjoyed her visit—she was a naturally positive person, and a lot of fun. We found a pleasant B&B in which she could stay, and included her in all the visits we made to friends and family. It turned out there was less time to privately see horse friends than we had anticipated, as

I was quickly reminded that family time in Denmark meant a return to the cholesterol-raising Danish "coffee table," but it was lovely seeing everyone.

But there were wonderful times as well. It was a happy day indeed when Birgit and I picked up our eight-week-old longhaired German Shepherd puppy. We had the time and a nice yard by the house to welcome our newest member of the family, Bjoern ("Bear").

Show season was approaching, and I remember Tanz was the first to go in one of the lower 4th-Level classes at a competition just south of Copenhagen. We finished second in a good-sized class and that was nice, but when I saw the horse who beat him, it was best that I kept my mouth shut, as I thought, *Hmm, I wonder if that was right...*

Birgit, who had done most of the training with her horse Waicon, was coming along well with him in his Grand Prix work. Our six-year-old Dutch horse was blossoming, and she had some very good wins at 4th Level at quite a big show in Holte, taking turns winning with another nice young horse owned by our friend Grethe, with Lone Madsen in the saddle. It was really special to compete at Holte again. The last class I had shown there was when I won the big Professional Riders' class where we exchanged horses in the fall of 1975, shortly before moving to America.

Tanzkoening was simply a blast to ride, with the most incredible uphill canter and super flying changes. I don't exaggerate when I say he had the potential to become a world-class horse, and even today, those lofty changes would easily have earned 8s and 9s across the board. At Holte, he gained attention by winning every 4th-Level class in which he was entered. I'll never forget that during the warm-up, I rode an extended canter, brought him back, and set him up for one of those enormous changes when Joergen Olsen, who used to work for me, commented, with his dry humor, "It was clean."

Grethe, who had been standing next to him, burst into laughter and confirmed, "Yes, it was!"

Debbie's horse, Wonderful, lived up to his name and started his winning streak at almost all the bigger Danish national shows. Next came a very large national show in Kolding, just north of where I grew up. We took only Wandi and Tanz to this show, and while Tanz handily won a class just below the Prix St Georges, Wandi won the Intermediare 2 the first time I showed him.

At these shows, podiums had been erected for first, second, and third-place riders in the center of the arena, and when obliged twice to stand upon the top of the podium for my wins, my eyes swept over the spectators and I caught sight of the faces of some of my friends who were watching the brief ceremony. Their expressions—or, it seemed to me, their lack of expression—puzzled me. No smiles, nothing. I immediately thought that, had this been America—where, let's face it, people whoop and cheer when a friend gets through their first 2nd-Level test—I would have been on the receiving end of pats on the back, thumbs up, and smiling congratulations. But here, that reserved Danish nature, whether meant to prevent me from getting a big head or simply encourage me to live my life under a cloak of humility, quickly served to remind me why I so enjoyed America. It's not that I was looking for adulation—it just might have been nice had someone said, "Well done."

I will say that I was given one positive experience in that show. My friend and colleague Ove Bisgaard, whom I had known in Denmark since returning from Germany at age 23, walked over to me, and in the most straightforward manner, said, *"Det er fand'me flot det du laver."* He used a swear word to describe his thoughts, and I guess today, his sentiments would be translated to something a bit coarse—"It's effing great, what you're doing." I have to say, it meant a lot to me, and it was the only direct compliment I received during our stay.

After Kolding, we went to two international shows, one in Sweden and one in Belgium, taking along Wonderful and Wandi, who finished with good placings in the Prix St Georges and Intermediare 1 and 2.

The last big national show was at home at Barthahus, just a few weeks before our return to the States. Debbie was there, along with Priscilla, and her friend Kerstin Christensen, widow of Walter Christensen. To cap off our stay at this facility, which held such cherished memories for us, was perfect. The show couldn't have gone better; both Tanz and Wonderful won their classes, and while I felt I was close to being able to ride a Grand Prix with Wandi, there was no Grand Prix listed in which to enter. I had inquired of management before the show whether I might be allowed to run through the Grand Prix test solely "hors concours," meaning "not for competition," so that I could see how Wandi would handle the test in a show atmosphere. They'd agreed, and I was satisfied with that.

The stands at Barthahus were pretty packed. My mind flashed back to when I had won the 6'4" high jump there, all those years ago. What a long way I'd come since that day...and thankfully, no beer crates were being used today! As I cantered around the arena once before going down the centerline, the announcer said loudly and clearly into the microphone, "And now, Gunnar Ostergaard will be performing a Grand Prix exhibition on Wandi."

What? That was news to me, and there was nothing I could do but go for it. As it turned out, my ride would actually be judged by a well-known, international Danish judge who rewarded me with a decent score that was not made public. Debbie, however, was delighted, and to this day I'm still not quite sure how to take Joergen Olsen's remark, in his trademark, dry style: "You are stealing all the ribbons."

To top off this memorable weekend, Priscilla Endicott swept all of us away for a marvelous dinner at Hornbaek's best restaurant, right on the ocean.

A few days before we left for the airport, Birgit and I held a sort of "thank you and goodbye" reception for all the morning riders with whom we had worked at Barthahus, and everyone seemed to enjoy themselves. We still laugh at the memory of a member of the barn staff who, on the morning of our departure when the horse van arrived, asked, "Are you going to take the puppy to America?" As if we'd even think of not bringing our Bear back with us!

How I wish I could say that everything I had hoped to share with my dear mentor Gunnar Andersen was possible. But it wasn't. Now 82, his longtime fear of becoming senile, as his twin sister had, was becoming a reality. I had so looked forward to him seeing our horses, but when we picked him up that particular April morning, outside his and Gerda's flat, he was making a bit of fun of us because we were wearing riding clothes—he had forgotten that we were going to the stable, and, thinking instead that we were going out to lunch, he was nicely dressed. However, once we arrived at the barn and got to the horses, his demeanor changed and he was more like his old self. As I trotted past on Tanz, he called out, "Ja, den kan gaa paa benene!"—"Yes, this one can move his legs!" His help from the ground certainly wasn't the same, but he was more than happy to take our lesson money—I mean that in the most endearing way, and we would have never taken that joy away from him.

The advancement of his dementia was breathtakingly quick. Gerda told me heartbreaking stories of him appearing in her bedroom at three in the morning, dressed in riding clothes and ready to go to the stable. He had no idea whether it was day or night. In August, toward the end of our stay in Denmark, he was admitted to a closed psychiatric unit at Hvidovre Hospital. Not long after his admission, I picked up Gerda one afternoon and we went to visit him. We had to wait quite a while to see him, and when we were finally allowed in, we found him to be well-groomed...and strapped to his bed. My heart broke in two as he lay there, speaking gibberish, completely unaware of his surroundings.

Anyone who has ever cared for someone with dementia knows it is one of life's most difficult challenges, and yet, in between the grief and the adjustments to a new "normal" time and time again, there can be moments of peace and even humor. Gerda told me there had been reports from the nurses that, from time to time, Gunnar would follow them with a broom and rap them on the backs of their legs, telling them to bend their knees and yelling, "More activity!" The thought of that, I have to admit, brings a smile, knowing he remembered his dressage career; but as I stood beside his bed in that psychiatric unit, all I felt was anguish.

After half an hour, Gerda took his hand and said, "We must be leaving now. You know Gunnar has to go back to America again soon." Suddenly, something changed in his eyes—a look of crystal-clear lucidity appeared. It was as if he recognized for the first time that it was me standing beside him, and, looking straight into my eyes, he said, "Please bring my best regards—I have so many friends in that wonderful country."

I cried. It was the last time I saw the man who had meant more to me in my professional life than anyone else.

CHAPTER
27

NO DRAMA AND NO REGRETS

W E WERE LOOKING FORWARD to returning to life in the States, and specifically to our winter season in Florida, particularly because we had had the opportunity to purchase a condo over which we had lusted. Like our other condo on Singer Island, right smack-dab on the ocean, this one had spectacular views, but from the eighth floor instead of the third. As with our smaller condo, this one offered a seascape of both the ocean and the Intercoastal Waterway, but even better, it comprised two joined flats on one floor, meaning we had far more room, not to mention a wraparound balcony. It never failed to amaze us to watch both the sunrise over the Atlantic and the sunset over the Intercoastal. Knowing this dream residence might be coming onto the market, as well as knowing Singer Island real estate was at a standstill during the summer months, we had given our realtor instructions to let us know should interest in the place increase. We got the phone call while we were still in Denmark, and we wired the deposit, as well as instructions to put our other condo on the market.

Purchasing this new residence, we knew, would make life a bit easier when we had guests. One of the things Birgit and I enjoyed was having the ability to give each set of parents an annual flight to Florida. They thought they had taken the express elevator to heaven, stepping off a plane into the subtropical climate after the endless cold and dark of Danish winter. This new condo would give us plenty of room to entertain, and entertainment was what our parents wanted! Besides the pool and the beach, they were eager to explore the local area, not quite taking in the fact that Birgit and I were working ten-hour days, and that wasn't even counting the forty-five minute commute each way. And so when we came through the door each evening, a bit worse for wear, there were our smiling parents, ready to party! Of course, we made the effort to give them the time of their lives. With two solid months of non-stop parents, we had seen them far more than we would have had we remained in Denmark—in other words, we had more of our parents than we could have ever dreamed!

Equine logistics and our lives in general continued seamlessly upon our arrival home, thanks to Tim Dutta. Our horses arrived comfortably from Denmark, coming in through New York, and were transported by van to Florida, where they reveled in the sparkling sunshine. Our training and competitive success seemed to snowball, and we had a terrific season.

In Venice, I rode Wonderful to victory in the biggest Prix St George class I had seen so far in the United States: sixty-seven horses! Tanz and Wandi continued their winning ways as well, collecting hatfuls of blue ribbons.

During this time, the best horse we owned was a spectacular gelding named after a famous French restaurant in Manhattan: Lutèce. Birgit gets much credit here, as she saw the potential that I couldn't in the two-year-old when we bought him. Prior to leaving for Denmark, he had been experiencing niggling lamenesses we couldn't quite figure out, and our plan was to simply turn him out for a year. Now, having returned, I put him back under saddle, and he blossomed in a big way. In the small tour, he won at Devon and the Festival of Champions, and that same year he was named USDF Prix St George Horse of the Year. He had an outstanding piaffe and passage, and all that needed to be confirmed were the one-tempi flying changes. It was heartbreaking when his lameness returned and was revealed to be navicular disease in both front feet. Lutèce then found a suitable and loving home at the farm of one of our clients.

By 1993, we had spent three summers in Vermont at Valerie's lovely barn, and were always grateful that she had put in those extra stalls just for us. Feeling that the board we had paid easily reciprocated her initial expense, not to mention the hour's drive, one-way, to and from the farm to our house, we began looking for another facility nearer to home.

There was, actually, a rather run-down place about a mile west of Chester, toward our main home, that we had seen from time to time. It had broken-down fencing and was desperately in need of painting, but the barn appeared solid, if with small stalls, and we had also been told that above it were three apartments. Best of all, it had an indoor 20 by 40-meter arena. While in Florida, we learned it had come onto the market and we were willing to take the risk. Calling our old friends the Schurinks, we asked if we could trouble them to go take a closer look, especially to assess the condition of the apartments. Their report was enthusiastic: "We could live there ourselves!"

We made a lowball offer, and it was nearly a month before the realtor phoned to give us the good news that it had been accepted. The thought of working just four miles from home was very attractive. There was so much more work we could do with those extra two hours that had been spent commuting each day. We were full of enthusiasm and couldn't wait to return, roll up our sleeves, and get to work.

Birgit arrived with the horses in the van before I did. I must stop briefly to point out that during all those years, she was an absolute star: each season, she did all the packing up, loading, and driving straight through between Vermont and Florida with her co-driver, Meri Strass.

Once in Florida, everything was unpacked and lugged over to the barn: the horses, feed, hay, tack, and equipment. I, despising those tasks, conveniently managed to schedule clinics just before the departure and arrival dates, working my way down and then back up the east coast. The excuse—and it was a valid one—was the income that would be generated.

Having once again unloaded and gotten the horses tucked in, Birgit phoned to say, "We have to do a lot of work, but a nice man dropped by to ask about arena time for his wife." This "nice man" would become my best male friend, until he died at the age of 70: Pat O'Connor. He and his wife, Mary Ann, became such close friends that they even began following us to Florida to escape the Vermont winters.

Pat had worked in property management for people with vacation homes. He had a background in construction, and offered his services if needed. Boy, did we. We knew upgrading the place would be pricey: we had to completely redo the footing in the indoor arena, as well as replace the kickboards. We had to build an outdoor arena, rebuild the barn, and turn those fifteen small stalls into ten large ones. The fencing needed to be torn down, and new fencing erected. Another barn—a small shed-row—was added outside, and we remodeled the upstairs apartments that would serve perfectly for two working students; above those, there was a third, which I would make into my office. And finally, everything needed to be repainted. We were hemorrhaging money and decided we needed to take out a mortgage; however, as there was no actual house on the property, this proved to be difficult.

In Chester, as in many a small town, rumor got around. In this case, word that we needed a mortgage spread, and the funniest variation on this rumor came from the owner of the local motel, called "Motel in the Meadow," and situated between our new facility and a dirt road where I often hacked our horses. One day at the grocery store, word got back to us that the motel owner had told fellow locals, "No wonder this guy can't get a mortgage—all he does is ride around on those beautiful horses all day!" In the end, we did secure a loan elsewhere, and we really enjoyed this third incarnation of Deerwood Farm—four miles from our Deerwood Farm home. It wasn't state-of-the-art, but it was functional, and positioned in a beautiful setting.

Meanwhile, in Florida, we enjoyed several happy years in our Singer Island condo, although I have to say, the one thing Birgit and I have always had in common is a love of the countryside. As appealing as an ocean view is, we simply began to miss the green, flowing landscape offered by terra firma. I'd begun teaching clinics in north central Florida, and found Ocala to be the sort of place I thought we both might like. It wasn't without risks—Ocala was quite rural in those days, and Birgit had voiced concerns that leaving the Wellington area also meant leaving our friends and the entire "Welly World" scene of lovely shops and restaurants. Indeed, it was a pleasurable lifestyle. But when we sat down and took into consideration that we were spending $30,000 each season to rent stabling in White Fences, as well as dealing with ever-increasing traffic congestion, it made sense to look further afield, among the rolling hills and native oak trees that made Ocala so enticing.

I had found a real estate brochure, and on the simple basis of liking the look of a married couple who were posing with their dog, I phoned the husband of this real estate couple, Steve Farrell, and left a message that we were "looking for twenty acres around Ocala."

Steve called back a little later and said, "My wife is into dressage, and wants to know if you are *the* Gunnar Ostergaard?" *The* Gunnar Ostergaard agreed that indeed I was, and the result was that Steve showed us several properties; but it was a 25-acre parcel, full of cows and nothing else, on which we made an offer in the end. It was going to be another undertaking that would require yet more elbow grease: we were going to have to build everything from the ground up, as it was simply raw land. But it was in a good location, and we really liked that there was a quiet, wooded area toward the back of the property, which would be a perfect site for a house. Birgit and I have always enjoyed having our privacy, away from our business, and this place ticked all the boxes.

Again, my dear friend Pat, who had been incredibly helpful with all the construction of our facility in Vermont, came to our rescue by flying down to Ocala. Staying for as long as it took, he oversaw every piece of construction: the building of the barn and working student apartment, fencing, and even making sure the power lines were buried to enhance the look of the place. It simply wouldn't have been possible to undertake such an overwhelming project without him, and he went out of his way to make sure we got the best possible result for the best possible price.

So efficient was he that after buying this cow pasture in the summer of 1999, by the following winter season of 2000, we had a barnful of clients, and never missed Wellington for a moment. Of course, we still went down for the shows, but we didn't miss living there. An added bonus was that my training business actually expanded, because for the first time, I began having clients who'd been unwilling to haul horses all the way to Wellington but were able to make the trip to Ocala from nearby southern states—and I, in turn, was now making comfortable drives to teach clinics I'd never been able to fit into my schedule before.

We had now contentedly entered middle age, and what followed were simply wonderful years with no drama and no regrets. We had our tranquil farm in the Green Mountains of Vermont that we loved, and a training facility that was a scant five minutes away. In Ocala, we had our winter farm and home. Birgit and I, at the end of a hard day, would sometimes catch ourselves and marvel over the fact that our lives continued to be full of great clients—many of whom were also good friends—not to mention wonderful horses to train, while teaching year-round in short sleeves. What could be better? We were even able to take regular short vacations to visit our home in Denmark. Yes, we had worked like Trojans to earn what we had, but it must be said that any serious horse trainer works hard, and yet things don't always go their way: horses go lame, clients change barns, and in the meantime, bills must be paid. Those things happened to us as well, and we just kept "thinking forward." Birgit and I have never taken any of our success for granted, and to this day, we are especially grateful we've been able to keep up the good health and abundance of energy required to do what we love.

CHAPTER
28

I CAN NEVER LOOK BACK

SOMETIMES I WONDER HOW MY LIFE might have gone had I not been able to bridle the two-year-old Jack, back when I was 12, at my Uncle Hans's farm. For sure, I was trying to escape my cousins' addiction to *Popular Mechanics* magazine and an army of cakes during that evening's coffee table, but I don't think it was a happy accident that I somehow managed to earn the trust of a wary young horse. In the end, everything has always been about the horses...and credit must also be given to my dear, tight-fisted father, who demanded I continue my lessons despite my first day's disaster at the riding school—so he could get his money's worth!

During those happy years commuting between Vermont and Florida, Birgit had the best Grand Prix horse that we had produced, after buying him as a six-year-old in Sweden. She earned a solid string of wins in big classes, and took the Grand Prix tri-color at the Southeastern States Championship held in Orlando. At this point in her life, Birgit wasn't super hungry to hit every show and rack up more wins. She was enjoying the daily journey of training and simply riding. It remains my view that they had the potential to go even farther, but I deferred to her decision. Birgit has always poured herself into the relationship she builds with each horse, and I'm glad she has.

In the meantime, I had produced Monhegan, a gelding I'd purchased as a five-year-old in Denmark. While he was not particularly strong in the hind leg, something between us clicked, and I had to have him. The fact that he was by Don Schufro might have played a small role. His road to Grand Prix was not easy, and I can still hear Birgit's voice, over and over, when I asked how his passage looked: "Un-level behind!" Yet every day, Monhegan asked, "What is next?" "What can I do better?" He was the same way at shows—he never looked right or left, and was simply the best worker bee, busily tackling everything asked of him. Because of this, I always rode him first or second each morning, and after dismounting, there wasn't a time when I didn't think, "What a great start to the day!"

Monhegan was no world-beater. He was my last Grand Prix horse (so far!), but he did win two national Grand Prix championships in 2010 and 2012 for (it's never easy for me to realize my age) the "Vintage Cup," which is for riders over 50. But what I remember best about Monhegan was the shared five minutes we spent together every day after work. He would look for me over his stall door, and like clock-work, I'd arrive with his daily apple. When I approached him, he would be wearing that kind, calm expression he always wore, and just seeing that relaxed me as well. Most horses will take a large chunk out of an apple and try to snatch the rest. Not my Monhegan. He would take the smallest bite and take his time chewing, blinking softly as if to say, "Let's just enjoy this time together." And we did. It was the best ten minutes of my day.

I am at a place in my life in which I feel I can say this: in our love for horses, Birgit and I have always trained fairly. Could we have become even more successful had we been "rougher and tougher" be-hind closed stable doors? Perhaps. But that sort of coarse approach, which, I am sad to say, I witnessed behind certain other closed doors—including from world-famous trainers in the most successful dres-sage countries—well, it grieves me to say that in training horses at the highest level, "the priest doesn't always practice as he preaches."

By 2006, changes were in the air even if some of them were seem-ingly the result of serendipity. One of them was the selling of our training facility just down the road from our Vermont farm. We hadn't really thought that much about it, until the owner of a local garage in Chester, Brian Benson, happened to be over one day repairing a piece of machinery. We liked Brian—the whole town did. He was what one might call a "salt of the earth" type of guy, who would go out of his way to help if anyone was in a bind, and he could fix anything. His wife, Kim, had an interest in horses, but I don't know if that was in his mind that day when he glanced up from the tractor he was working on and toward the hills of our 27-acre farm, and said in his unmistakable Vermont dialect, "Would be a nice place to put a house up there in them hills."

Half in jest, I replied, "Yes—do you want to buy it?"

When he answered, "Maybe," I thought for a moment.

"Could we keep a barnful of horses here each summer?"

Brian didn't hesitate. Smiling broadly, he said, "Sure!"

It took three dinners in our log and stone farmhouse (and I won't divulge how many beers went with them) until we had a deal in place. Birgit and I couldn't believe it. We had, in honesty, spoken about slowing down a little, but we had been mostly kidding when we had. Mostly. But now life had become even better, as we would keep our training and competition schedules between Chester and Ocala without the worry of maintaining the upkeep of our Chester farm. And yet, we would still be able to use and enjoy all the improvements we'd made!

By the time 2010 rolled around, Birgit and I began to think about spending more time in Denmark, as we were now in our sixties. It made sense to finally let go of our Manhattan apartment, which we had owned for twenty-five years. We weren't getting to New York very much, and I'd actually made a sweet deal with each of the two tenants who had lived there all that time. For a reduction in rent, it was agreed that I could stay there while in the area teaching clinics. The tenants were enthusiastic, I was able to enjoy my beloved city after work, and the extra reward was that when it sold in 2013, I was told it sold for more than any other apartment in the building.

We started looking at houses in Denmark, and decided to settle near Copenhagen. I had seen a farm on the island of Funen online, and remarked, "This is beautiful, but do we really want to live on this island?" It turns out that we did. We viewed five or six places, but that one stole our hearts. We hadn't even seen the house, just the property in its breathtaking setting; and just as Birgit had done all those years ago in Vermont, I drank in the view and said, "I think we should live here."

The idea was that we would reside at our Danish farm permanently, with the exception of my returning to the States to continue teaching clinics. We bought it that summer, and by winter the following year we had two containers shipped to Denmark from Vermont and Florida, carrying two John Deere tractors, furniture, and an old Jaguar. While that might sound extravagant to some, let me assure you that shipping was far less expensive than attempting to replace those belongings in Denmark!

Once we had let go of our Chester facility, it was not only time to bid goodbye to our Ocala farm, but to our private Vermont residence as well. Selling the Ocala farm was logical: we were no longer training and competing as we had done in the past. And while it wasn't an easy decision, it made no sense to retain our Vermont home, so dear to our hearts for decades. The only time I was going to Vermont was to teach clinics—hardly a reason to keep and maintain a property of that size. To be completely honest, it had been for sale, on and off, for years, but it was the Covid pandemic that inspired a former Boston city dweller to put in the offer we ultimately accepted.

Fortunately, Birgit and I were in a position where we could wait as long as it took to sell both farms. We put a substantial price on the Ocala farm and were prepared to wait—and wait we did. It took two years before we sold it. Now, all I had to do was to find an American base to purchase for my trips back across the Atlantic.

It felt natural that, as we'd been the first dressage trainers who had taken a string of horses to Wellington, we would look there for our winter home, keeping our summers in Denmark. Finding a small home in the vicinity, I gave it my best shot from 2015 to 2017, but it simply didn't feel comfortable. I don't know if it was because Wellington had changed or I had—perhaps a combination of the two—but I knew I hadn't found home. Florida felt too hot, and if the point of living in Wellington was to go to the shows, well, I have to say, Denmark had far more to offer in that regard. A relatively short drive would take me to Germany, for example, as well as other European shows, to see the top riders and horses in the world, rather than the same faces I was seeing week after week in Florida.

In all those years that I taught clinics organized by my good friend Martha Kemmer in Columbus, North Carolina, perhaps it should have occurred to me to drive ten minutes into historic downtown Tryon, soaked in elegant equestrian history and dotted with both charming "arts and crafts" cottages and lovely estates. But I didn't! Instead, I drove north to Hendersonville, Brevard, and Blowing Rock, looking at property around there. I even returned to New York, in Millbrook—which is gorgeous, but with those winters, I might as well have kept the Vermont farm. It took until 2017 for me to begin to explore around Tryon, and when the World Equestrian Games came to the newly constructed Tryon International Equestrian Center in 2018, I'd bought my house, two minutes from downtown. I have to say I have never felt as comfortable anywhere as I do in this friendly little village. From the first day I set foot in Tryon—as I did in America itself, that very first day in 1975—I knew I was home. The kindness of neighbors, as well as strangers; the encouragement; the enthusiasm...I can never look back.

It's perhaps a little too appropriate that my last name, Ostergaard, translates in English to "eastern farm," and of course my lifelong passion for real estate didn't end with my Tryon house. While I might have traded in the Green Mountains of Vermont for the Blue Ridge Mountains of Tryon, I needed one more Deerwood—and chose acreage twenty minutes away in Mill Spring, very close to beautiful Lake Lure, North Carolina. After a life of going non-stop, it is in this partially wooded countryside that I can relax and read a book—until I have to leave to teach my next clinic!

People have asked me why, at the age of 77, I continue to teach as much as I do. The answer is that it defines me. It's who I am. Whether I am teaching a 68-year-old woman on a 22-year-old horse, or an up-and-coming young rider on a spectacular prospect, I have always done my best—in all three countries I've worked in. There's a saying: to be happy in life, do what you love and make it your career. And in doing that, there has been an abundance of joy, as my sweetest memories are not so much the championships I've won or the pleasant lifestyle Birgit and I achieved, but instead the moments that would make any committed horseman smile: hacking out in the field in Vermont, riding the first one-tempi flying changes on a horse I've produced, or simply leaning against the stall door in the evening light, sharing silent, heartfelt communication with a beloved horse over an apple.

All those years ago, it began with a young boy in his bedroom, reading and dreaming about settlers forging a life in the prairies and woodlands of a far-flung country called America. I'm no longer a young boy, but the wonder and romance I felt then for this country has steadfastly remained. And always will.